Laura **Clyde** Shannon **West**

NEW Pass Trinity
Student's Book

Trinity Grades ISE II

7-8

contents

	Page	Grammar (G) & Functions (F)	Phonology
GRADE 7			
UNIT 1 National & local produce & products			
	8	Modals & phrases for expressing future possibility & uncertainty (G & F)	Showing uncertainty
UNIT 2 Education			
	14	Modals & phrases for giving advice & making suggestions (G & F)	Word Stress Modal verbs
UNIT 3 Early memories			
	20	*Used to* for describing past habits (G & F)	Interpreting intonation *Used to*
Review units 1-3	26		
UNIT 4 Village & city life			
	28	Second conditional (G). Expressing agreement & disagreement (F)	Subject-area vocabulary Weak forms & contractions
UNIT 5 National customs			
	34	Relative clauses (G). Eliciting further ideas & expansion of ideas & opinions (F)	–
UNIT 6 Recycling & pollution			
	40	Simple passive (G) Discourse connectors (G)	–
Review units 4-6	46		
GRADE 8			
UNIT 7 National environmental concerns			
	48	Third conditional (G) Expressing Impossibility (F)	Contractions & weak forms in conditional sentences
UNIT 8 Personal values & ideas			
	54	Linking words & phrases (G) Persuading & discouraging (F)	–
UNIT 9 Public figures			
	60	Past Perfect (G)	Intonation in questions
Review units 7-9	66		
UNIT 10 Society & living standards			
	68	Reported speech for reporting the conversations of others (G & F)	Connected speech
UNIT 11 The world of work			
	74	Present Perfect Continuous (G) Expressing feelings (F)	Stress & intonation to indicate emotion
UNIT 12 Unexplained phenomena & events			
	80	Expressions for speculating and expressing doubt (G & F)	Using sentence stress to speculate
Review units 10-12	86		

Contents

Exam expert Topic (T) & Conversation (C)	Exam expert Interactive (I)	Writing
Exam advice (T)	Introduction to the phase	Exam & portfolio practice
Choosing a topic (T) Exam practice (C)	Keeping the conversation going	Exam & portfolio practice
Making notes for your topic (T)	Identifying key words in a prompt	Exam & portfolio practice
Making notes (T)	Exam advice & practice	Exam & portfolio practice
–	Asking for further information	Exam & portfolio practice
Concerns about your topic (T) Asking questions (C)	Taking control over the interaction	Exam & portfolio practice
Introduction to the phase (T) Exam Practice (C)	Introduction to the phase	Exam & portfolio practice
Choosing a topic (T)	Exam practice	Exam & portfolio practice
Using mind maps (T) Responding appropriately (C)	Keeping the conversation going	Exam & portfolio practice
Maintaining the interaction (T & C)	Maintaining the interaction	Exam & portfolio practice
Anticipating & answering questions (T)	Taking control over the interaction	Exam & portfolio practice
More concerns about your topic (T) Keeping the conversation going (C)	Encouraging comments	Exam & portfolio practice

Trinity Grades 7-8 Overview	4	Writing File	92
Diagnostic Test	6	Appendix 1: Portfolio Feedback Form	110
Trinity Takeaway	88	Appendix 2: Grading & Marks	111

exam overview

TRINITY GRADED EXAMINATIONS IN SPOKEN ENGLISH (GESE), GRADES 7 AND 8, AND INTEGRATED SKILLS IN ENGLISH (ISE), LEVEL II

GESE Grades 7 & 8 (CEFR B2)

Time: 15 minutes

Format and procedure:

1. Discussion of a **topic prepared by the candidate** (up to 5 minutes)
- **Communicate facts and opinions** about a chosen topic and **engage the examiner in discussion** of it.
- **Ask and answer questions** about the topic, giving explanations or clarifying when requested.
2. **Interactive task** (up to 4 minutes)
- **Take control** over the interaction and **maintain the conversation**.
- **Use language functions** of the relevant grade when appropriate.
3. Conversation on **two subject areas selected by the examiner** (up to 5 minutes)
- **Answer the examiner appropriately** to show understanding.
- **Share responsibility for the maintenance of the interaction** with the examiner.

Grade 7 exam syllabus:

Grammar
- second conditional
- simple passive
- *used to*
- relative clauses
- modals and phrases used to give advice and make suggestions, e.g. *should/ought to, could…*
- modals and phrases used to express possibility and uncertainty, e.g. *may, might…*

Subject areas for Conversation phase
- education
- national costumes
- village and city life
- national and local produce and products
- early memories
- pollution and recycling

Functions
- advantages and disadvantages
- making suggestions
- describing past habits
- expressing possibility and uncertainty
- eliciting further information and expansion of ideas and opinions
- expressing agreement and disagreement

Phonology
- correct pronunciation of words relevant to the vocabulary for this grade
- rising intonation to indicate interest and surprise as appropriate
- falling intonation to indicate the end of a turn
- intonation and features of connected speech beyond sentence level

Exam overview

Grade 8 exam syllabus:

Grammar
- third conditional
- Present Perfect Continuous tense
- Past Perfect tense
- reported speech
- linking expressions, e.g. *although*...
- cohesive devices, e.g. *so to continue*...

Subject areas for Conversation phase
- society and living standards
- personal values and ideas
- the world of work
- unexplained phenomena and events
- national environmental concerns
- public figures past and present

Functions
- expressing feelings and emotions
- expressing impossibility
- reporting the conversations of others
- speculating
- persuading and discouraging

Phonology
- correct pronunciation of words relevant to the vocabulary for this grade
- intonation to give up and offer turns
- stress, intonation and pitch relevant to the language functions listed above

ISE II

Portfolio Tasks

Format:
- **Candidates must complete one task from each section** (see below) during class time or individual study. The tasks must be selected from the list for the current year found on the Trinity College website.

Section 1 (120-150 words)
correspondence task
e.g. letter, email

Section 2 (170-200 words)
factual writing task
e.g. report, article, review

Section 3 (170-200 words)
creative/descriptive task
e.g. diary, story, description

Controlled Written examination

Time: 2 hours
Format:
- Candidates must complete both tasks on this exam paper. No choice of tasks is given.

Task 1
Reading into writing (250 words): you read a text and then complete a task based on information from the text

Task 2
Writing task (250 words): a similar task to those required in the portfolio but without extra support material

The interview

Time: 12 minutes
Format:
- Discussion of a **topic prepared by the candidate** (up to 4 minutes)
- **Interactive task** (up to 4 minutes)
- Conversation with the examiner **including a discussion of the portfolio and one subject area from Grade 8 list selected by the examiner** (up to 4 minutes)

Diagnostic test

Listen to the examiner asking some questions and choose the best answer, A, B or C. There is only one right answer for each question. You will hear each question only ONCE. Good luck!

1
 A Because I want to have a certificate.
 B Because of a certificate.
 C Because I will practise.

2
 A I was here two years ago.
 B I've been here for two years.
 C I will be here for two years.

3
 A Yes, I do.
 B I prefer to travel by a car.
 C I prefer to travel by car.

4
 A I won't be sure.
 B I thought I like coffee.
 C I think I'll go for a coffee.

5
 A No, I haven't.
 B No, I didn't.
 C No, I never tasted it.

6
 A since I was 12
 B I want to study for years.
 C Because it's useful.

7
 A I'll teach maths.
 B I like to teach maths.
 C I'd like to teach maths.

8
 A on 25 December
 B Presents are exchanged and lots of food is eaten!
 C For two days!

9
 A No, I don't like dance music.
 B I like music that makes me dance.
 C Yes, I love music!

10
 A I used to live in a small village, too.
 B I like villages better.
 C Was it nice?

11
 A I agree.
 B They never do in my country.
 C No, they should never punish them.

12
 A Well, natural resources might last longer.
 B Well, natural resources can last longer.
 C Well, natural resources must last longer.

13
 A In case I need it in my future career.
 B Because I have two lessons every week.
 C In case of travelling to England.

14
 A So what?
 B What for?
 C Really? What else do you do?

15
 A So have I.
 B I agree completely.
 C That's wrong.

16
 A I'd like to send my friends emails more easily.
 B I have wanted to send my friends emails.
 C I would have sent a lot of emails to my friends.

17
 A It used to be very dirty. Now it's cleaner.
 B In case it was dirty.
 C Yes, it has.

18
 A I had more free time.
 B I will have more free time.
 C I might have more free time.

19
 A Tell something more!
 B Go on, tell me more!
 C Why did you do that?

20
 A Do you agree that recycling rubbish is a good idea?
 B Have you agree that recycling rubbish is a good idea?
 C Must you agreed that recycling rubbish is a good idea?

21
 A What did your parents do if you'd pass all your exams?
 B What will your parents do if you will pass all your exams?
 C What would your parents do if you passed all your exams?

22
 A What do they celebrate St Valentine's Day?
 B Is St Valentine's Day celebrated in your country?
 C How often do they celebrate St Valentine Day?

Diagnostic test

23
- A Well, I guess people would have been poorer.
- B Well, I suppose people will be poorer.
- C Well, I imagine people are poorer.

24
- A Well, I have improved.
- B Well, I've been studying hard.
- C Well, I will study hard.

25
- A Not really, she finished studying when she got married.
- B Not really, she finished studying when she had got married.
- C Not really, she had finished studying when she got married.

26
- A You told me that before.
- B Because of my religion.
- C I said earlier that I didn't believe in ghosts.

27
- A The Prime Minister – in other words the person who governs the country.
- B I met Nelson Mandela once.
- C probably not

28
- A I suppose so.
- B They haven't done so.
- C Goodness! That would be wonderful!

29
- A I wouldn't do that if I were you.
- B When did you give it?
- C Oh, I'm sorry!

30
- A Of course I did!
- B Yes, twice! But nobody believes me.
- C They are very frightening!

31
- A You're right, she never performed in Italy before last night.
- B You're right, she was never performing in Italy before last night.
- C You're right, she had never performed in Italy before last night.

32
- A He is talking about the economy.
- B He had told the truth.
- C He said that living standards had improved in the last 5 years.

33
- A I don't – unless the crime is really horrible.
- B I don't – except the crime is really horrible.
- C Because some crimes are really horrible.

34
- A I don't believe it!
- B I won't believe you!
- C That isn't believable!

35
- A You must not to use your car.
- B I wouldn't use the car if I were you.
- C You shouldn't have used your car.

36
- A Do you think the next Prime Minister is a woman?
- B Is it likely to have a woman Prime Minister?
- C Might the next Prime Minister be a woman?

37
- A Has life expectancy become more?
- B Has life expectancy enlarged?
- C Has life expectancy increased?

38
- A Can you tell me what are your ambitions?
- B Can you tell me what your ambitions are?
- C What ambitions can you have? Tell me.

UNIT 1
National & local produce & products

Vocabulary

1a Work with a partner. Match the names of the products (1-5) with the photos (A-E).

1 maple syrup
2 tulips
3 balsamic vinegar
4 caviar
5 amber

b 🎧3 Listen to Anna and Tim talking about where they think the products and produce in a) are from. Match the photos (A-E) to the countries (1-8) according to what they say. There are three extra countries.

1 ☐ Canada
2 ☐ China
3 ☐ Holland
4 ☐ Iran
5 ☐ Italy
6 ☐ Russia
7 ☐ France
8 ☐ USA

c 🎧3 Anna and Tim are unsure about some of their answers. Listen again and complete the sentences from their conversation.

1 **Anna**: Well, I'm ...., but I think it .... be Canada.

2 **Anna**: ...My brother wouldn't know – he .... have a .... about things like that!

3 **Anna**: I'm ...., but I think they .... produce it in France. Or, actually, ... not – .... it's Italy. What do you think?

4 **Tim**: Um, I'm .... not .... Let's leave that one for now.

5 **Anna**: ...the amber – I'm not ...., but it .... be Iran.

6 **Tim**: Well, I've .... no .... myself, so let's put that!

8

National & local produce & products

Grammar focus

Expressing present and future possibility and uncertainty

1 Modal verbs – *could/may/might* + infinitive
It **could be** Canada.
It **may be** the USA.
They **might produce** it in France.
Do you think it **may/might/could be** Iran?

2 Adverbs *maybe* and *perhaps*
Or, actually, **maybe** not.
Perhaps it's Italy.

3 Other expressions of uncertainty

uncertain

I'm not sure.
I'm not certain.
I'm not completely sure.
I'm really not sure.
I've got no idea.
He doesn't have a clue about things like that!

more uncertain

2a Work with a partner. Ask and answer questions about where the products in exercise 1a) are from. Use the language for expressing possibility and uncertainty from the Grammar focus.

A: Do you think maple syrup comes from Canada?
B: Maybe, but I'm not certain. It could be the United States. What do you think?
A: I haven't got a clue, actually!

b Check your answers with your teacher.

c Work with a partner. Ask and answer questions about your experience of the products and produce in exercise 1a).

Have you ever tried maple syrup?
What was it like? Did you like it? Why/Why not?
Where did you buy it?

Phonology

Showing uncertainty

3a (4) Listen to the sentences and underline the word with the main stress in the sentences.

0   They <u>could</u> be.
1   They may be.
2   They might be.
3   I'm not sure.
4   I'm not completely sure.
5   I'm really not sure.
6   I've no idea.
7   I haven't got a clue.
8   Perhaps you're right.

b Now mark where the speaker's voice goes up (↗) or down (↘).

c (4) Listen again and repeat the sentences using the same stress and intonation.

UNIT 1

Vocabulary

5a Work with a partner. Make a list of the different types of places for going food shopping.

E.g. supermarkets

b Using your list from a), tell your partner which is your favourite and least favourite type of place for food shopping.

I really like going to the market near my house – it has lots of fruit and vegetables and they're really fresh and cheap.

I hate going to big supermarkets outside town. They're too big and there's too much to choose from!

Reading

6a Work with a partner. Which countries do you associate with these food products?

0	beef	USA, Argentina
1	tomatoes	....
2	potatoes	....
3	broccoli	....
4	bananas	....
5	carrots	....
6	lamb	....

b With your partner, make a list of some advantages for buying local food products instead of products that have come from another region or from abroad.

E.g. Local products are fresher.

c Read the article. Check your answers to a) and compare your list from b) with the information given in the text.

d Work with a partner. Ask and answer these questions about food products.

1. What food items are produced in your area? Are these products exported to other regions and/or abroad?
2. Which local food products do you/your family buy?
3. Is it possible to buy out-of-season food products where you live? Do you/your family ever buy them? Why/Why not?
4. Do you/your family worry about food miles when shopping?

Writing

ISE Reading into Writing

➡ *See Writing file on pages 92–109.*

7 Write a report (approximately 250 words) for an online magazine for young people:

i) summarising in your own words what the text says about food miles and ways to reduce them **and**

ii) suggesting ways of educating people about the problem.

National & local produce & products

LONG-DISTANCE FOOD

How many 'food miles' have you consumed today? Or, to put it another way, how much air pollution has been created by getting the food to your table? These statistics about food imports to the UK – all of which, apart from bananas, can be produced in Britain – might cause a few surprises.

- Two thirds of tomatoes consumed in the UK are imported from Saudi Arabia – **3,100 food miles**.
- 350,000 tonnes of potatoes are imported into Britain every year, many of them from Israel – **2,200 food miles**.
- Broccoli grows in the UK from February to April, but it is available there all year round. It is imported mainly from Spain – **730 food miles**.
- India is one of the main producers of bananas, along with Ecuador, Costa Rica, the Philippines, and Colombia. India to UK: **5,106 food miles**.
- China is one of the world's largest producers of carrots, followed by Russia and the USA. However, in the UK, most of the carrots come from South Africa – **6,000 food miles**.
- The UK is the biggest importer of lamb from New Zealand – **11,700 food miles**.

Bringing food such long distances is bad for the environment – and it's not good news for our health, either. Food that has come this far may be days or weeks old, and the older the fruit or vegetables, the fewer vitamins remain in them. So what can we do to reduce our food miles? Here are some simple steps you can take:

- Buy foods that are grown and produced locally whenever you can, including meat and dairy products.
- Do your food shopping at farm shops and farmers' markets.
- Eat seasonal foods – don't expect to be able to eat everything all year round.

exam expert

Interactive phase

Introduction to the phase

8a 🎧5 Listen to the candidate describing the Interactive phase to a friend and choose the correct answers in the sentences.

1 It tests the candidate's ability to *maintain/finish* conversations.
2 It lasts for about *4/6* minutes.
3 It is started by the examiner *asking a question/making a statement*.
4 The *examiner/candidate* is responsible for keeping the conversation going.
5 If the candidate does not participate, the examiner *will/won't* help keep the conversation going.
6 After the examiner starts talking the conversation *can go in any direction the candidate chooses/goes in a set direction*.

b 🎧6 Look at these strategies for keeping a conversation going. Listen to the examples (1-5) of the candidate keeping different conversations going. Write the number of the example next to the correct strategy (A-E).

A [1] Checking that you have understood.
B [   ] Asking questions to find out more information.
C [   ] Showing interest in what the person is saying.
D [   ] Telling a similar story about yourself or someone you know.
E [   ] Summarising what the person has said.

c Work with a partner. One of you is Student A, the other Student B. Follow the instructions.

Student A

Stage 1 You're the examiner, Student B is the candidate. Start the Interactive task with the following statement: *I have to go to a wedding next weekend, but I have nothing to wear.*

Stage 2 You're the candidate, Student B is the examiner. Listen to the examiner's statement, then respond by using the strategies from b). Try and keep the conversation going for four minutes.

Stage 3 Decide with Student B what went well in the conversations and what you could improve. Your teacher will also give you some ideas.

Stage 4 Repeat Stage 1 with the following statement: *I have so much work to do. My boss gives me too much to do. I work late every evening.*

Stage 5 Repeat Stage 2.

Student B

Stage 1 You're the candidate, Student A is the examiner. Listen to the examiner's statement, then respond by using the strategies from b). Try and keep the conversation going for four minutes.

Stage 2 You're the examiner, Student A is the candidate. Start the Interactive task with the following statement: *I have to take a really difficult exam next week.*

Stage 3 Decide with Student A what went well in the conversations and what you could improve. Your teacher will also give you some ideas.

Stage 4 Repeat Stage 1.

Stage 5 Repeat Stage 2 with the following statement: *I'm really bored where I live. There's nothing to do.*

d Change roles and repeat stages 1-2.

exam expert

Topic phase
Exam advice

9a Complete the advice (1-8) about the Topic phase with *do* or *don't*.

0 *Do* choose a topic that you are interested in and know a lot about.
1 .... choose a topic from the Subject areas for your grade.
2 .... prepare a speech – this phase should involve a **discussion** about the topic between you and the examiner.
3 .... prepare enough material to talk for up to five minutes for the graded exams (four minutes for ISE II).
4 .... use notes and/or diagrams to help you.
5 .... let the examiner have a copy of your notes (but the notes are not assessed).
6 .... anticipate questions the examiner might ask you about your topic, and think about possible answers.
7 .... be prepared to explain in more detail what you have said if the examiner asks you to.
8 .... bring anything that's alive to the exam, e.g. insects or animals!

b Think about a presentation you have seen in the past, e.g. at school, at work, on TV, and make notes in answer to these questions.

1 What was the presentation about?
2 Was it well organised?
3 Was it interesting? Why/Why not?
4 Did the presenter use notes and/or diagrams to explain things?
5 Did the presenter ask the audience questions?
6 What could the presenter have done to improve their presentation?

c Work with a partner. Tell each other about the presentation that you made notes on in b), then decide on the two most important things to do in a presentation, and the two most important things not to do.

Writing

ISE Portfolio/CW

➡ *See Writing file on pages 92-109.*

10 Choose one, or more, of these writing tasks.

Correspondence (ISE II 2010)
A television company wants to make a documentary about local products. Write an email to the producer of the programme telling her about a famous product from your area. Explain how it is made and say how it would benefit your area if it was featured on the programme.

Factual writing
Write an article for an online magazine explaining why people in your area are starting to buy more locally produced food products.

Creative/descriptive writing
Write a story for a writing competition about a young woman who became a millionaire by inventing a product that was sold successfully in her own country and abroad.

Trinity TAKE AWAY

Examiner: Do you think that in the future we'll only eat fruit and vegetables *grown* in our own country?
Candidate: I'm *not sure* but we may eat *more* local produce in the future than we do now. It *might be* difficult to change people's eating habits though.

UNIT 2
Education

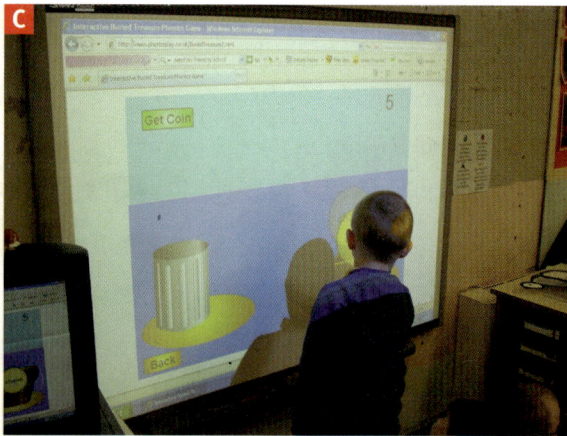

Vocabulary

1a In pairs, look at the pictures. How is technology being used for education? Have you ever studied in these ways?

b In your opinion are the following advantages (A) or disadvantages (D) of studying and learning with technology? Compare your ideas with a partner.

1. ☐ You can study from home or work.
2. ☐ You have to buy equipment.
3. ☐ Connection speeds can be different.
4. ☐ You can access a wide range of information and resources.
5. ☐ You need to learn new skills to take part.
6. ☐ Some people don't have access.

Reading

2a Read the article on the next page about the use of technology in education. Decide if the eight phrases in italics are true in your experience. Then compare your thoughts with a partner.

b Match each of these headings to a paragraph in the article. There is one extra heading.

A Things to celebrate
B Making the classroom international
C The down side
D A new skill we all need
E A positive revolution?

Education

Classrooms go digital

1 ☐ Worldwide, a digital revolution is going on in classrooms. Many Ministries of Education are adopting technology as an essential part of the development and delivery of education. But is this actually helping?

2 ☐ There are many studies that show that the use of technology ¹*improves motivation*, ²*provides exposure to the real world* and ³*makes the abstract visible*. This last point is put forward frequently for subjects like science and mathematics. Many teachers report that the use of applications like Excel, simulations and interactive diagrams bring maths and science alive. Technology also ⁴*helps to individualise learning* making it easier to appeal to different abilities in one class.

3 ☐ However, for all the positive studies there are also those that say that the use of technology ⁵*has no effect on educational attainment*. Many studies conclude that students aren't getting better assessment results and this has led some schools to abandon the use of laptops. Teachers have had to adapt ⁶*to learn new skills* and sometimes ⁷*gain a new qualification*, which has been costly. Not only have they had to learn how to use the technology but also to adapt to the changing nature of their role: from an expert or instructor to a facilitator.

4 ☐ For all the disagreement, there seems to be one point of agreement. With the rapidly growing number of authors and the ease of publishing content online, all students have had to ⁸*learn how to assess the authority of information*. You really can't believe everything you read these days and before using a reference, students need to be able to assess if an information source is reliable.

Writing

ISE Reading into Writing

➡ *See Writing file on pages 92–109.*

3 Refer to the article. Write an article (approx. 250 words) for a school magazine:

  i) summarising what the article says about technology and education **and**

  ii) offering some advice to people studying in this way.

Vocabulary

4a 🎧 **7** Complete the table with the different forms of the words from the text, like in the example. Listen and check your answers.

b 🎧 **8** Complete the sentences with a form of the word in brackets. Listen and check.

1 It is important that employees are both experienced and ………………. . (*qualify*)
2 How many ………………. are there at your school? (*study*)
3 How long have you been ………………. English? (*learn*)
4 I almost crashed the car in my driving lesson last night. The ………………. was a bit shocked. (*instruct*)
5 People 50 years ago weren't as well-………………. as we are today. (*educate*)

	verb	abstract noun	person	adjective		verb	abstract noun	person	adjective
0	authorise	authority	author	authoritative					
1		education			**5**			student	
2		information			**6**	learn			–
3			instructor		**7**			teacher	–
4		assessment		–	**8**		qualification		–

UNIT 2

c What are the differences between the teaching-related words below? Consider when we use these words, what the person does, where they work or what they teach. Work in small groups. Use a dictionary to help you if you need to.

> tutor   coach   instructor   teacher   professor
> headmaster   dean   examiner

E.g. I'm not completely sure but I think a 'coach' is for someone who teaches sport.
Doesn't a 'dean' work at a university?

Phonology

Word stress

5a Mark the word stress on each word like the example in the table in exercise 4a). Then listen to the words and check if you are correct. In the example the word stress changes depending on the word form. Which other words in the table also change like this?

b Listen to the words that end in -*tion*. What is common about the word stress in these words?

Listening

6a Listen to a candidate talking about studying online. Read the advice for online learners below. Put a tick (✓) next to the advice that the candidate mentions, then check with your partner.

1. ☐ Print out the course notes and readings.
2. ☐ Contact your tutor immediately if you are having trouble.
3. ☐ Use the chat rooms and message boards as much as possible.
4. ☐ Make sure you're a self-motivated learner.
5. ☐ Check what technical specifications your computer should have before starting.
6. ☐ Take a test to see if you are suited to online learning before starting.

b Complete the sentences below with the exact words the learner says. Then listen and check your answers.

1. She's just six months old, and I really ………… ………… ………… all my time with her.
2. I just go there at the beginning of each course and download the articles or print them. ………… ………… ………… ………… ………… ………… them as you can't read for too long on screen.
3. Also, you ………… ………… it if you haven't got a pretty good computer and Internet connection. Some of the articles take ages to download. If you aren't sure, you ………… ………… the university.

Education

Grammar focus

Giving advice and making suggestions

The most common way to give advice is with **should/should not/shouldn't** + infinitive without *to*.
You **should** ask the teacher. You **shouldn't** study all night just before an exam.
Do you think I should take an evening course after work?

To give strong advice we can use **ought to** + infinitive without *to*.
You really **ought to** be sure you need a qualification before studying for it.

It is very rare to use *ought to* in the negative form. We use *shouldn't* instead.
You ~~oughtn't to~~ **shouldn't** study so late. You have school tomorrow.

Other ways to give advice and make suggestions include…

1 it is (not) **a good idea** + infinitive with *to*
It's a good idea to find a study partner if you are a social learner.
It's not a very good idea to… Do you think **it's a good idea to**…?

2 If I were you, I would/would not + infinitive without *to*
If I were you, I'd send an email to other people in the class and ask them.
I wouldn't spend too much time on it **if I were you**.

3 could + infinitive without *to*
You could ask them if they have organic ingredients.

4 you'd better + infinitive without *to*
You'd better ask somebody for the notes from the lesson you missed.

5 How/What about + verb + *-ing*…? **Why don't you** + verb…?
How/what about taking your clothes to a charity shop?
Why don't you ask before you go ahead?

6 try in a question: *try* + verb + *-ing*
Have you tried keeping a vocabulary diary of new words?

7a Expand these sentences into advice. Check your answers with a partner.

1. should/check/how much/costs/before/order/online
2. not/good/idea/study/online/if/not/very/motivated
3. would/not/borrow/money/go/holiday/if/were you
4. ought to/call/boss/if/not/go/to work
5. had/better/make/booking/because/restaurant/always/busy
6. have/try/talk/her/instead/ignore/her

b In pairs, write advice or suggestions for these situations, using the forms above.

1. Your brother has been offered two different jobs, but is not sure which one to take. One pays more but it's a long commute. The other pays less but is in the same town.
2. Your neighbour is thinking of having a lunchtime party, but does not know what food to make. It's summer and it will probably be outside.
3. Your friend wants to recycle more.
4. Your mother has a terrible headache.

UNIT 2

Phonology

Modal verbs

8a 🔊(13) Listen to how the modal verbs are pronounced in these sentences. What do you notice about the last sound of the modal verb?

1. I might eat and study or do it on the train, or on holidays.
2. She gives us news there and tells us where we should be up to in our reading.
3. Also, you shouldn't do it if you haven't got a pretty good computer and internet connection.
4. Some of the articles take ages to download. If you aren't sure, you should ask the university.
5. There are lots of people working full-time who wouldn't be able to attend classes if they had to go to the university.

What happens when the word after the modal verb starts with a vowel sound? What happens if it is a consonant sound?

b In pairs, practise saying these sentences.

1. They wouldn't ask if they already knew.
2. She shouldn't go out alone so late.
3. Why should I wait for her? She never waits for me.
4. I'd be so angry if it were me.
5. He could work hard all day and he never got tired.
6. I might go. I'm not sure yet.

🔊(14) Now listen to the sentences. How did your pronunciation compare to the model?

exam expert

Interactive phase

Keeping the conversation going

9a Keep the conversation going in the Interactive Task by asking questions. Match these questions with what you want to know.

A probability/likelihood   E size
B duration since last time   F hour
C recommended action   G duration
D quantity/price   H frequency

1. ☐ What time does class start?
2. ☐ When did you last study online?
3. ☐ How often do you go to school?
4. ☐ How big is your class?
5. ☐ How likely is it that he'll fail?
6. ☐ What do you think I should do?
7. ☐ How much does the course cost?
8. ☐ How long does your lecture last?

b Your teacher will give you a topic and start a conversation. In groups write some questions and pass them to another team. Now check the questions the other team wrote and give them suggestions. Then play the game again.

Conversation phase

Exam practice

10a Which type of school did you study at/are you studying at? What is the difference between the types of school below?

1. co-educational/single-sex school
2. private/state school
3. religious/non-religious (secular) school
4. academically-oriented/artistic or sports-oriented school
5. large school with many students/small school with few students

exam expert

b Discuss the advantages and disadvantages of these different types of schools.

Private schools are expensive, but they probably have excellent facilities.

c In pairs, give some advice to the following families about the best types of schools for them. Use the Grammar focus on page 17.

1. Family 1 – 5 children, of different ages and genders.
2. Family 2 – 1 son, loves to play sport.
3. Family 3 – 3 daughters.
4. Family 4 – 2 children, one boy and one girl, from a Muslim family.

Topic phase
Choosing a topic

11a In teams, write a list of topics in five minutes. Choose six or seven to talk about.

b Ask yourself the questions below for the topics you chose and write Y (yes) or N (no). If you answer 'yes' for all eight questions, then it could be a good one for you.

1. ☐ Am I really interested in this topic?
2. ☐ Will I be able to talk about this topic comfortably in English?
3. ☐ Do I know the vocabulary and grammar relevant to this topic?
4. ☐ Will I be able to answer questions about this topic confidently?
5. ☐ Will I have enough to say about this topic to speak for up to five minutes?

c Choose a topic from your list. In pairs, discuss the topic. How much can you say about it now?

d In pairs, decide how the discussions went. What went well? What could be improved?

Writing
ISE Portfolio/CW

➡ *See Writing file on pages 92-109.*

12 Choose one, or more, of these writing tasks.

Correspondence (*ISE II 2008*)

Your English friend has decided to go backpacking for a year on her own, but her family are totally against the idea and would prefer her to go to university. Write a letter to your friend discussing the advantages and disadvantages of her plans and giving her some advice about what to do.

Factual writing (*ISE II 2007*)

Your school/workplace is thinking of introducing some online language courses to help people improve their English. Write a report for your teacher/manager stating the advantages and disadvantages of this method of learning a language compared with more traditional methods.

Creative/descriptive writing (*ISE II 2008*)

Write a short story for a writing competition that begins with the words, 'What should I do? She'd made me promise not to tell anyone, but this would be difficult to keep secret'. Now finish the story.

Examiner: What advice would you give to someone learning English?
Candidate: Well, they **should** study hard of course. But they **shouldn't** just rely on their classes. Visiting a place where people speak English *is a good idea*.

UNIT 3
Early memories

A
B
C
D
E

Listening

1a Look at the photos of people's earliest memories. What do you think happened? Discuss them with a partner.

b 🎧 Listen to five people talking about their earliest memories. Match each story to one of the photos. How many of your predictions were right?

Vocabulary

2a Choose the word that best completes each sentence. If you are not sure, try to guess.

1 I remember *go/going* to the supermarket, but I don't remember *buy/buying* that ice cream.
2 I *vividly/totally* remember our first house. It was on a big hill.
3 I *completely/distinctly* remember leaving my keys here. How strange that they aren't here.
4 I'm so sorry. I *absolutely/completely* forgot it was your birthday today.
5 My *earliest/youngest* memory is of my dad smiling at me while I was in bed.
6 I have *kind/fond* memories of my grandparents. They were lovely people.

b 🎧 Listen again. Check your answers to a) by finding a similar example in each conversation.

Early memories

c Complete the sentences with these words.

*completely remember clearly vaguely
long-term bad forget memorise*

1. That was such a horrible time. I wish I could ……………… it.
2. I ……………… the day when my uncle got married. It was the first time I saw him in a suit.
3. The one thing that I ……………… remember is the smell of the roses. I can smell them now just thinking about it.
4. I'm really nervous about the test. Last night I tried to ……………… everything, but I can't remember anything now.
5. I'm not sure now. I ……………… remember you telling me something about it.
6. After he was hit on the head he ……………… forgot everything. He can't even remember where he lives.
7. My grandmother has a really good ……………… memory, but she sometimes doesn't remember things from yesterday.
8. I'm sorry, I have a really ……………… memory for names. What was your name again?

d Work with a partner and follow these instructions.

1. Choose four expressions from a) and c), and write them down.
2. Think of something that happened to you in the last seven days.
3. Plan how you can tell your story using your chosen expressions. Make short notes if you need to.
4. Now give your notes to a partner so they know which words you want to practise.
5. Tell your story. Your partner should make sure you use all four chosen expressions.
6. Listen to your partner's feedback about how well you used the expressions you planned to.

Phonology

Interpreting intonation

3a (16) Listen to parts of the conversations about memories again. Decide if the listener is asking for more information (A) or showing surprise and interest (S). One of the conversations has both.

1 ☐   3 ☐   5 ☐
2 ☐   4 ☐

b (17) You can show interest and encourage someone to keep talking by asking questions. Listen to some examples from a). Write down the questions you hear.

1 A ………………………………………………
  B ………………………………………………
2 A ………………………………………………
  B ………………………………………………

c Practise asking for more information in pairs.

Student A: Tell a story but stop now and again and wait for your partner to ask a question. Then answer and continue your story and stop again. Continue until you have finished your story.

Student B: when your partner stops speaking, use the cards your teacher gives you to ask a question and keep your partner going. Can you use all your cards?

Once you have finished, swap roles.

UNIT 3

Grammar focus

Used to for past habits

There are several ways we can talk about habits in the past:

1 *used to* + infinitive without *to*, or *did not use to* + infinitive without *to*
We use this to talk about:
a something we often did in the past but we do not do anymore.
I **used to visit** my grandparents every weekend.
b a state that lasted for some time in the past.
We **didn't use to** live near the city centre.

2 *would* + infinitive without *to*, or *would not* + infinitive without *to*
We use this to talk about something we often did in the past but do not do now. In spoken English we usually use the contractions *'d* and *wouldn't*.
She**'d** swim for hours, until it was almost dark.

3 We cannot use *would* to talk about states in the past. We use *used to*.
~~We'd live in an old house on Smith Street.~~ We **used to live** in an old house in Smith Street.

4 For questions, we usually use *use to* instead of *would*.
~~Where would you play when you were a boy?~~ Where **did** you **use to play** when you were a boy?

5 When we tell a story about past habits, we often start with *used to* and continue with *would*.
We **used to go** skiing at Christmas. We**'d get up** early in the morning and open our presents, and then we**'d go** straight outside in the snow to make a snowman.

6 It is common to use adverbs of frequency (e.g. *always, never, often, usually*) with *used to* and *would*.
We**'d always enjoy** the ride home. We **never used to do** that when I was young.

4a Complete the sentences with the correct form of *used to*, followed by the verb in brackets.

1 Why .... going to the cinema? Don't you enjoy scary films? (*like*)
2 I .... physics until my last year at school. Then I didn't understand anything. (*love*)
3 .... you .... in the school football team? (*play*)
4 Where .... your parents .... before they bought their business? (*work*)
5 I recognise him. He .... us to see that band we liked every week years ago. (*come with*)
6 I .... so tall, you know. I was the shortest in my class at primary school. (*be*)

b Underline the correct form, *used to* or *would*. In which sentences are both possible?

1 They *would/used to* walk to school because they didn't have a car.
2 We *would/used to* play football in the street every night in summer.
3 I *would/used to* be the tallest boy in my class at primary school.
4 She *would/used to* have really long hair before she cut it.
5 Didn't you *use to/Wouldn't you* live on Ford Street a few years ago?

Early memories

c Complete the gaps in the story with *used to* or *didn't use to*.

> I'll never forget those summer weekends in Australia. They were such wonderful times. I ¹............... live in a country town, which was about 30 minutes from the sea. I ²............... live in the city like I do now. We ³............... have a car then so we went by bus. We ⁴............... stay in a camping ground and the first thing we ⁵............... do was put on our swim suits and run into the sea. Our friends next door ⁶............... come with us each day for a walk to the pier. One of my favourite parts of the day was when we ⁷............... go to the corner store that was air-conditioned and get an ice-cream. I ⁸............... like going back into the heat again.

d Now replace some of the words with *would* (*'d*) and *would not* (*wouldn't*) and some adverbs of frequency (e.g. *always, never, often, usually*) to make it sound more natural.

Phonology

Used to

5a (18) Listen to these sentences. What do you notice about the pronunciation of *used to* and *didn't use to*?

1. We always used to enjoy ourselves.
2. I didn't use to like school when I was a child.
3. He used to play basketball with my brother.
4. Did you use to go to school with my sister?
5. They didn't use to eat much when they were small.

Now practise saying the sentences.

b In pairs, practise reading out the story from exercise 4d). Note any places where your partner could improve their pronunciation. Swap roles and try again.

c (19) Now listen to the story. Compare your pronunciation with the model. Give yourself a mark out of 10 for your pronunciation of *used to*.

Intonation for interest and surprise

6a (20) Listen to these examples and write down the words that are repeated to show interest and surprise. Does the intonation rise or fall at the end?

1 ....
2 ....

b (21) Listen to six funny experiences that people have had. What word or words would you choose to repeat to show interest or surprise? Write the words down and compare with a partner. Then practise saying them with the right intonation.

c Tell your partner about something funny that has happened to you or someone you know. Listen to other people's stories and show surprise by repeating a word or words they have used. Be sure to use the right intonation. Who had the funniest story in the class?

exam expert

Topic phase

Making notes for your topic

> When you are preparing for your topic it is helpful to take notes. You can show how different aspects of the topics are related and it can help you remember what you'd like to talk about. You can take short notes into the exam with you.

7a Read this article about memory. Imagine you are going to use it as the basis for research into your topic presentation. Make notes as you read. Compare your ideas with a partner.

b Imagine you are going to talk about the article below for your topic presentation and then tell your own earliest memory. Make notes about your memory to add to your notes from a).

c Find a partner and share your ideas from the article and your earliest memories. Are there any common elements to your memories?

Writing

ISE Reading into Writing

➡ *See Writing file on pages 92-109.*

8 Now write an article (approximately 250 words) for a school magazine:

i) summarising in your own words what the article says about memory **and**

ii) discussing the methods you use to remember things.

Children remember more than we first thought

Short and long-term

Our memory is perhaps our defining human characteristic. It is the basis for learning and growth, helping us to improve and develop. Many people know of two types of memory: short-term and long-term. Short-term memory is the basis of our working memory when we are drawing on a number of memories to do the task in hand. Long-term memory stores facts, events and knowledge and helps us deal with things that are happening now and to plan for the future. However, there are other types of memory.

Narrative and emotion

Our memory for chronological events and narrative develops between the ages of two and four. This would seem to correspond with many people's experience. For most people, their earliest memory is usually when they are about two or three years old. However, there are other memories that we all have from a much earlier age. Our memory for feeling and emotion is fully developed when we are born. We are not able to relate these feelings or emotions to events and stories, but that does not mean we cannot remember. This emotional memory is not remembered with our minds but with our hearts, body and stomach. So just as a baby may remember the love of its parents, she or he will also remember emotions of fear or panic.

Working independently

All of these types of memory can work independently of each other. For example, there are reports of people with brain damage and no long-term memory, physically reacting to doctors that had administered unpleasant tests.

Interactive phase

Identifying key words in a prompt

The Interactive Task starts with a prompt (statement) from the examiner. After that it is your responsibility to take control of the conversation. If you identify a few words in the prompt that are important, it will give you some ideas about where the conversation can go. If you run out of things to say from one question, you can ask another one to start a new conversation from the same prompt.

9a Look at the prompt below and underline the important words that you could base a conversation on.

> 'I'm making an important speech next week. I'm a bit nervous about it.'

b Look at the questions below and match them to a part of the prompt.

1. What's the speech about? ....
2. Why is the speech so important? ....
3. Why are you worried? ....
4. What day next week? ....
5. Who will be listening to the speech? ....
6. Why were you chosen to make it? ....

c Listen to your teacher saying some prompts. In pairs write down the key words and then write some questions for each key word. How many questions can you write?

d Now practise with a partner using the prompts from your teacher and the questions you wrote. Time your conversation. Can you speak for four minutes?

Writing

ISE Portfolio/CW

➡ *See Writing file on pages 92-109.*

10 Choose one, or more, of these writing tasks.

Correspondence *(ISE II 2009)*
You were delighted to receive a letter from an old friend. He used to live in your area, but you have not seen him for many years. Write a reply to your friend telling him about the changes that have taken place in your area and recalling some of the activities you used to enjoy doing together.

Factual writing *(ISE II 2011)*
You recently read your grandmother's diary from when she was a teenager. Write an article for a history magazine explaining when the diary was written and describing some of the things your grandmother used to do. Say whether you would have liked to be a teenager at that time.

Creative/descriptive writing *(ISE II 2011)*
Write a description for a family magazine of a place you used to visit as a child that has special associations for you. Describe the place, say what you used to do there and explain why it is so memorable.

Examiner: So what about you? What was it like where you grew up?
Candidate: Well... there wasn't much to do around where I lived. But that didn't stop us from having fun. On the weekend we **used to** disappear in the mornings on our bikes and **wouldn't** come back until dark.

Review Units 1-3

1 Complete the sentences with the words in the box.

> could be to practise may scratch
> used to have 'm not sure 'd climb
> shouldn't eat 'd take ought to see
> might come

1. It's cold out. If I were you, I .... a hat and scarf.
2. It's a good idea .... before your writing test.
3. I've never seen it before. I .... where it came from.
4. He's not sure if he can make it to the party. He said he ....
5. When I lived in Rome I .... an espresso every day at 11.
6. The baby .... asleep right now. You should send a text and ask when it's best to call.
7. You .... a doctor if your sore throat gets worse.
8. Be careful of the cat. It .... you.
9. You .... so much cream. You'll feel sick!
10. I remember going on holiday to the mountains when I was small. We .... for hours every day.

2 Complete the text below with the vocabulary and expressions provided. You will not need to use all of them.

> Fiat 500s I'm not sure might have been
> Minis stayed used to find used to got up to
> used to stay used to allow used to travel
> vividly remember were allowed

I [1].................. the things we [2].................. on vacation when I was younger. My family [3].................. to Italy for summer every year. We were fascinated by the different things we [4].................. there. For example, there were very few [5].................. where we lived, but we saw people driving them everywhere in Italy. My brother and I thought they were cute and wanted to have one as our first car. [6].................. why we liked them so much. It [7].................. because they were so small. One year we [8].................. on a farm and they had a Fiat 500 in one of the fields. My brother and I [9].................. drive it. We had so much fun.

3 Complete the sentences so they are true for you. Compare your ideas with a partner. Were any of your sentences similar?

1. I may .... this weekend. I'm not sure.
2. The weather? It's likely to .... tomorrow.
3. If you are not happy with something you have bought, you should ....
4. You really ought to .... if you feel ill.
5. My earliest memory is ....
6. When I was small I used to ....

Review units 1-3

What do you remember about the Topic phase of the exam?

4 Are the following statements true or false? Can you correct the false ones?

1 There is a list of topics that you must choose from.
2 You can take things into the Topic phase to talk about e.g. photos.
3 You cannot take in any notes, diagrams or mind maps on your topic.
4 The examiner will ask questions so you have to be prepared to talk about your topic in depth.
5 You are expected to lead the topic phase, not the examiner.
6 The Topic phase lasts no longer than 5 minutes.
7 The examiner is not allowed to interrupt you or ask for clarification until the end.
8 You must choose a topic that is different from the subject areas of the course book.
9 You should try and use the grammar and language from the course in your topic.
10 If you have a prepared speech, you will make a bad impression and may effect your grade.

Exam tips – Topic phase

1 Take in something physical, such as a photo related to your topic. Something that you can both see can provide good support if you get stuck.

2 Don't rehearse too much. The examiner can easily hear if you have learned exactly what you are going to say and will stop you by interrupting and changing focus.

Units 1-3 Self-evaluation

Write Y (yes) or N (needs more practice) for each statement.

1 ☐ I can talk about national and local produce and products.
2 ☐ I can talk about education.
3 ☐ I can talk about memories and things I remember.
4 ☐ I can express present and future possibility and uncertainty.
5 ☐ I can use different forms to give advice and make suggestions.
6 ☐ I can use different forms for talking about habits in the past.

Now you write 'can do' statements like the ones above for the interactive and communicative skills you have practised in Units 1-3.

UNIT 4
Village & city life

Vocabulary

1 Match the places (1-4) with the photos (A-D).

1. a town
2. a village
3. a city
4. the countryside

Phonology

■ Subject-area vocabulary

2a Listen to the words from exercise 1, then answer the questions.

1. Are the letters *ow* in *town* pronounced /aʊ/ or /əʊ/?
2. Are the letters *age* in *village* pronounced /ɪdʒ/ or /eɪdʒ/?
3. Are the letters *ci* in *city* pronounced /tʃɪ/ or /sɪ/?
4. Are the letters *ou* in *countryside* pronounced /ʌ/ or /aʊ/?

b Listen again and repeat.

c Work with a partner and ask and answer the questions about where you live.

1. What type of place do you live in?
2. What do/don't you like about the place you live?

> I live in a village. I like the fact that it's easy to get around – you can walk everywhere – but I don't like the fact that there's nothing for young people to do in the evenings.

Village & city life

Reading

3a Match the headings (A-E) to the blogs (1-5) about life in a village.

- A ☐ crime
- B ☐ natural surroundings
- C ☐ entertainment
- D ☐ transport
- E ☐ shopping

b Read the blogs again. Are the statements true (T) or false (F)?

1. ☐ It's difficult to get to places if you don't have a car.
2. ☐ There isn't anywhere to buy food in the village.
3. ☐ Entertainment in the village is limited.
4. ☐ Crime is a problem in the village.
5. ☐ The natural surroundings in the village are helpful for jim@tilford's work.

4a Work with a partner. Make a list of the advantages and disadvantages of living in a village. Use ideas from exercise 2 and add any more you can think of.

Advantages	Disadvantages
It's peaceful.	Public transport not usually very good.

b With the same partner, list the advantages and disadvantages of city living.

Advantages	Disadvantages
There's lots to do.	It's noisy.

c Change partners and compare your ideas from a) and b).

There's lots more entertainment in a city. That's important to me, as I love going to the cinema. I go at least three times a week. I couldn't do that in a village.

www.tilford.net

1 jb@tilford
You can't get anywhere from here if you haven't got a car. They closed the train station years ago. There are buses to the nearest town, but only two a day – and the last one back is 6 p.m.!

2 sara88@tilford
We're lucky – we've got a car and can go into town to the big supermarket there. We wouldn't starve if we didn't have a car, because there's a small general store in the village. But it doesn't have much choice – and we'd spend more money, because it's not cheap.

3 Aec47@tilford
There's a pub and that's it, really! If you want to go to the cinema, or to a restaurant, you have to go into town. But there are other things to do here – you can go for nice long walks in the countryside, or cycling. It depends what you're into, really.

4 pp@tilford
What I really like is that it's so safe here. I can leave my house unlocked without any worries. And my car, too. If I lived in a city, I couldn't do that.

5 jim@tilford
I love the fact that it's so quiet here – no loud traffic, like in towns and cities, just the sound of the birds! I used to live in London and there was always noise. The peace here is just what I need for the kind of work I do. It's also very beautiful. It's so nice to look out of your window and see trees and flowers.

Writing

ISE Reading into Writing

➡ *See Writing file on pages 92-109.*

5 Read the blog posts in exercise 3 again, then write an article (approx. 250 words) for an online environmental magazine:

i) summarising in your own words what the blogs says about life in villages **and**

ii) comparing this way of life with the situation where you live.

29

UNIT 4

Grammar focus

The second conditional

1 To talk about unlikely or imaginary present or future situations and their present or future consequences, we use the second conditional:
If + past tense + 'd/would + infinitive.

We use *would* when we feel sure about the consequence:
We **wouldn't starve if** we **didn't have** a car.
If we **did** all our food shopping in the village, we**'d spend** more money.

We use *could* to talk about ability = would be able to:
If I **lived** in a city, I **couldn't** do that.

We use *might* when we're not sure about the consequence:
If he **lived** in the country, he **might** feel lonely.

2 We make questions with the second conditional like this:
(question word/s +) *would* + subject + infinitive, *if* + subject + past tense
OR
If + subject + past tense, (question word/s +) *would* + infinitive
Would you **live** in a city **if** you **didn't have** children?
How often **would** you **go** to the cinema **if** you **lived** in a village?
If you **had** lots of money, **would** you **buy** a big house in the countryside?

6a Complete the sentences using the words and phrases from the box.

> 'd go   'd live   could pass   didn't have
> didn't work   didn't have to   do   won
> worked   would   might feel

1 If I .... the lottery, I .... travelling for a year.
2 What .... you .... if you .... work?
3 We .... in a city if we .... children. I really miss city life.
4 He .... his exams if he .... harder, but he doesn't study at all.
5 If I .... so much, I .... less tired in the evenings.

b Complete these second conditional sentences with your own ideas.

1 If I had so much money that I never had to work, I ....
2 If I could choose where to live, I ....
3 If I could change something in the world, I ....
4 If I was the President/Prime Minister of my country, I ....

c Work with a partner. Find out how your partner completed the sentences in b) and ask for more information about your partner's answers.

A: If you had so much money that you never had to work, what would you do?
B: I think I'd still work. I'd try and become a writer if I didn't have to worry about money.
A: Really? What kinds of things would you write?
B: Fiction. The kinds of things that I like reading.

Village & city life

Phonology

■ Weak forms and contractions in second conditional sentences

7a (23) Listen to the sentences (1-4) and write the number of words you hear. Contractions count as two words.

1 ....   3 ....
2 ....   4 ....

b (23) Listen again and write the sentences. Underline the stressed syllables.

c (23) Listen again and repeat.

Listening

8a (24) Juliet is talking to her friend Tom about moving from the city to a village. Listen and tick the points they mention, then compare your answers with your partner's.

1 ☐ quality of life
2 ☐ the natural environment
3 ☐ housing
4 ☐ entertainment
5 ☐ ethnic diversity
6 ☐ commuting
7 ☐ crime
8 ☐ community spirit

b (24) Listen again and circle the point/s in a) that Juliet and Tom completely agree on, then compare your answers with your partner.

c (24) Listen again and complete the expressions for agreeing and disagreeing from the conversation.

1 **Tom**: Well, yes, I agree .... you to a ...., but it depends on your definition of 'quality of life', doesn't it?
2 **Juliet**: I don't .... that. It depends on what you're interested in doing, surely?
3 **Tom**: Well, yes, I .... your ...., but I like the kind of things that the city has to offer...
4 **Juliet**: Yes, that's ....
5 **Juliet**: Yes, you're .... that...
6 **Tom**: I .... you're .... that...

Function focus
Expressing agreement and disagreement
Full agreement
(Yes,) you're right (about that).
I agree completely.
I couldn't agree more.
(Yes,) that's true.
Full disagreement
(I think) you're wrong (about that).
I don't think that's right.
(I'm afraid) I disagree completely.
Some agreement
(Well, yes,) I agree with you to a certain extent, but...
(Well, yes,) I see your point, but...
Some disagreement
I don't know (about that).
I'm not sure (about that).
I'm not sure that I agree (with you).

exam expert

Interactive phase

■ Exam advice & practice

9a Complete the advice about the Interactive phase using the words in the box.

> ask   explain   opinion   say

In this part of the exam the examiner may give an ¹............... to start the conversation.

You need to:
- ²............... if you agree or disagree;
- ³............... why you agree or disagree;
- ⁴............... the examiner a related question.

b One of you is Student A, the other Student B. Read your rolecards and follow the instructions.

Student A

Stage 1 You're the examiner, Student B is the candidate. Give an opinion about **quality of life** in a village. Respond to the question that the candidate asks you.

Stage 2 You're the candidate Student A is the examiner. Agree or disagree with the opinion that the examiner gives. Give reasons why, then ask the examiner a related question.

Stage 3 Repeat Stages 1 and 2 twice. Give opinions about **entertainment** and **the natural environment** in a village.

Student B

Stage 1 You're the candidate, Student B is the examiner. Agree or disagree with the opinion that the examiner gives. Give reasons why, then ask the examiner a related question.

Stage 2 You're the examiner, Student B is the candidate. Give an opinion about **transport** in a village. Respond to the question that the candidate asks you.

Stage 3 Repeat Stages 1 and 2 twice. Give opinions about **community spirit** and **crime** in a village.

Topic phase

■ Making notes

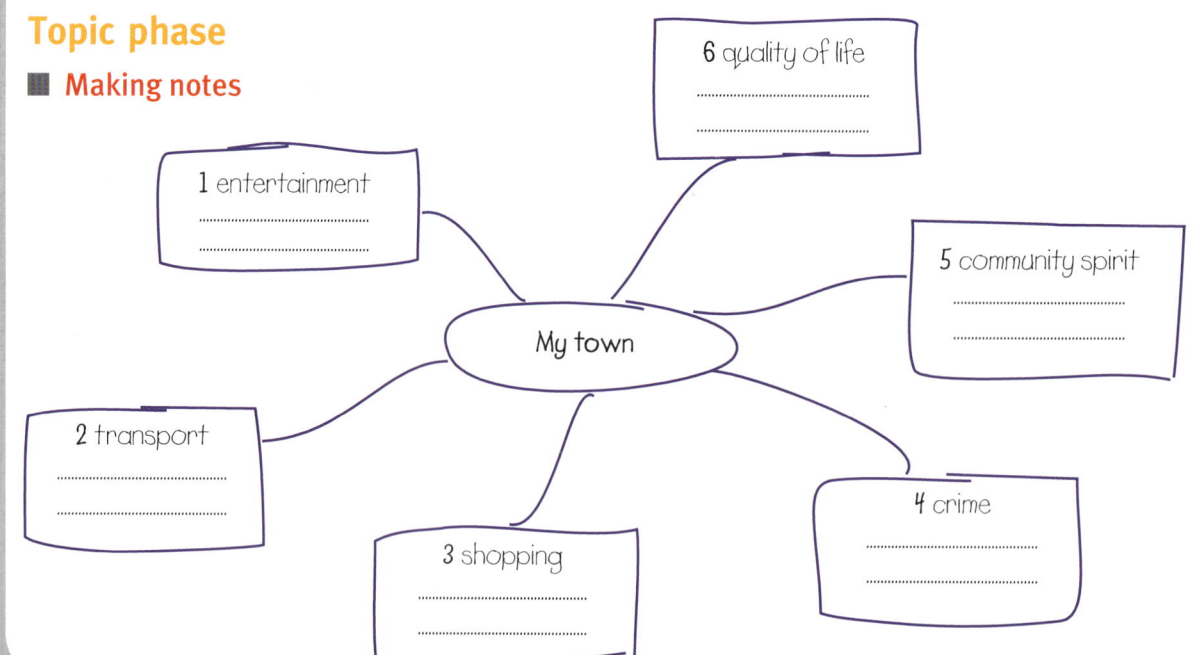

exam expert

10a Match the candidate's notes (A–C) about life in their town to three of the points on their mind map on page 32.

> A excellent underground – lots of lines
> good bus service – frequent, efficient
> driving a nightmare – heavy traffic, expensive to park
>
> B safe in centre
> problems on outskirts of city, poorer areas
>
> C my area, people don't help each other much neighbours not very friendly

b Write notes for the three remaining points on the mind map. Invent information as necessary.

c Work with a partner and compare your notes from b). Add any new ideas to your notes.

d Take it in turns to lead a 5-minute discussion using your notes from c).

Writing

ISE Portfolio/CW

➡ See Writing file on pages 92-109.

11 Choose one, or more, of these writing tasks.

Correspondence (*ISE II 2010*)
Your friend recently moved from a flat in the city to a farm in the countryside. She is finding the change difficult and feels lonely. Write an email to your friend, encouraging her to see the positive sides of country life and suggesting ways in which she could meet new people.

Factual writing
You would like to persuade more people to move to your village. Write a report for a community group explaining the advantages of living in a village and suggesting ways of persuading people to move there.

Creative/descriptive writing (*ISE II 2011*)
Last week you moved from a small village to a big city. Write your diary explaining how your life has changed and describing how you have been feeling. Speculate as to whether or not you will enjoy city life.

Examiner: I think there's much better quality of life in a village than in a city.
Candidate: Well, **I'm not sure about that**. I think it depends what you're into. **The natural surroundings in a village can be beautiful**, and there's not usually much crime, but **in a city there's much more to do**.

UNIT 5
National customs

Vocabulary

1a Match the festivals (1-6) to the photos (A-F).

1. Carnival
2. Divali: Hindu Festival of Light
3. Festival of the Autumn Moon
4. Halloween
5. New Year
6. Thanksgiving

b Work in pairs. Answer these questions about each of the festivals in a).

1. Where is the festival celebrated?
2. Which time of year is it celebrated?
3. What's the idea behind the festival?
4. How is it celebrated?

c Ask your teacher about any of the festivals in a) that you aren't familiar with.

d Answer these questions with your partner.

1. Are the festivals in the pictures a custom where you live? How do you and your family celebrate them?
2. What other festivals do you and your family celebrate?

National customs

Listening

2a Work with a partner. Decide how customs connected with these aspects of life (1-5) could be difficult for someone from another country.

1. food
2. religion
3. timetables
4. clothes
5. topics of conversation

b 🎧25 Listen to Emily, a British woman, talking about her experiences of other national customs. Tick (✓) the aspects of life in a) that she mentions.

c 🎧25 Listen again and say if the statements (1-6) are true (T) or false (F).

0	T	Emily found the early start to the day in Mexico difficult.
1	☐	She always used to go to bed early in Mexico.
2	☐	She found mealtimes too early in Spain.
3	☐	She now agrees with Italians about when to drink certain types of coffee.
4	☐	She only experienced carnival in Italy.
5	☐	Carnival is a custom in the UK.
6	☐	Emily has celebrated carnival in two places in Italy.

d Discuss these questions with your partner.

1. Which customs in your country do people from abroad enjoy?
2. Which aspects of life in your country might be difficult for people from another country?
3. Have you ever been to a country where you found certain aspects of life difficult?

I think people from another country would really enjoy our custom of big, long lunches!

Everything starts late in the evening here – if you go to a party, it doesn't start until 10 p.m. That might be difficult for people from another country.

I found shop closing times difficult in the UK – in the smaller towns, everywhere closes so early, at around 5.30pm.

3 🎧25 Listen to the interview with Emily again and complete the sentences from the conversation.

1. Do you .... specific customs, ... the way of life in general?
2. Well, it would be .... to .... what you have to say about both.
3. And .... in other countries?
4. Anyway .... eating, was there .... to .... customs about food itself that you found difficult...?
5. Can you .... us something .... what this custom ....?

Function focus
Eliciting further information & expansion of ideas and opinions

(Can you) **tell me/us** (something/more) **about** what it involves?

Do you mean... (or)...?

(And) **what about**...?

It would be interesting to hear/know what you think about...?

Talking about food/customs, **was there anything to do with this/these that you: could tell me/us more about?**
found/think is difficult/interesting?

35

exam expert

Interactive phase

■ Asking for further information

4a Work with a partner. Identify words/phrases in the examiner's prompt to ask for more information about.

Last year, I went to Venezuela and saw an interesting festival.

b  Listen to an examiner and candidate having a conversation based on the prompt in a). How many questions does the candidate ask the examiner?

c  Listen again and write down the questions.

d One of you is Student A, the other Student B. Read your rolecards and follow the instructions.

Student A

Stage 1 You're the examiner, Student B is the candidate. Use the prompt from a) to start a conversation. Respond to the questions that the candidate asks you using information from the recording in b).

Stage 2 You're the candidate, Student B is the examiner. Develop a conversation from the examiner's prompt, using language from the Function focus to ask for further information.

Stage 3 Decide with Student B what went well in the conversation and what you could improve. Your teacher will also give you some ideas.

Stage 4 You're the examiner, Student B is the candidate. Use the prompt below to start a conversation, then respond to the questions that the candidate asks you.

Prompt
I went to a Halloween party last weekend. It wasn't very exciting.

Stage 5 Repeat Stage 3.

Stage 6 Repeat Stage 2.

Student B

Stage 1 You're the candidate, Student B is the examiner. Use your questions from c) and the language from the Function focus to develop a conversation in response to the examiner's prompt.

Stage 2 You're the examiner, Student A is the candidate. Use the prompt to start a conversation, then respond to the questions that the candidate asks you.

Prompt
We went to Brazil for carnival last year. It was great but really expensive.

Stage 3 Decide with Student A what went well in the conversation and what you could improve. Your teacher will also give you some ideas.

Stage 4 You're the candidate, Student A is the examiner. Develop a conversation from the examiner's prompt, using language from the Function focus to ask for further information.

Stage 5 Repeat Stage 3.

Stage 6 Repeat Stage 2 with the prompt:

I usually spend New Year with my family, but this year I've booked to go away and I'm feeling a bit worried.

National customs

Grammar focus

Relative clauses

There are two types of relative clauses:

1 Defining relative clauses are used to give essential extra information. Without this information the sentence would not make sense.
*I had classes **that started at 7a.m!***
*...it meant **that I had to get up at 5.30.***

2 Non-defining relative clauses are used to give non-essential extra information. The sentence would still make sense without this information.
*Coming from Britain, **where it's normal practice to have dinner much earlier**, I found this a bit difficult at first.*
*I went to the carnival celebration in Viareggio, **which is also quite famous in Italy**.*

Relative pronouns are used to connect relative clauses.

Defining relative clauses		Non-defining relative clauses	
that or **which** to talk about things	**that** sounds more informal than **which** or **who**	**which** to talk about things	you can't use *that* in this type of relative clause
that or **who** to talk about people		**who** to talk about people	
when to talk about times/periods		**when** to talk about times/periods	
where to talk about places		**where** to talk about places	

5a Complete the sentences with a relative pronoun from the Grammar focus.

1 It's the festival in December .... people give and receive presents.
2 He's the man .... lives in the big house at the end of the street.
3 What are some of the customs .... you like most in your country?
4 In Spain, ... people have lunch very late, it's normal to have dinner at 10 p.m.
5 She got her degree at the London School of Economics, ... is one of the colleges of London University.
6 He's marrying a woman called Luz, ... comes from Argentina.

b Join the sentences using a defining or non-defining relative clause.

1 Carnival is a festival. It's held in Spring.
2 Divali is held in India in October or November. It is a two-day festival, celebrated with lights and fireworks.
3 Thanksgiving is a day of celebration. It is held in the US on the last Thursday in November.
4 Christmas pudding is a dessert made with dried fruit and nuts. It's eaten on Christmas Day.
5 I come from France. We eat dinner at around 7.30 p.m.
6 He's the American man. He goes to the Venice Carnival every year.

UNIT 5

Reading

6a Work with a partner. Answer these questions about national customs to do with food.

1. What customs are there in your country associated with food?
2. Are there any foods associated with certain festivals?
3. Make a list of any unusual festivals that involve food, in your country or abroad.

b Now read the excerpt from an article about unusual festivals around the world that involve food. Are any of the festivals the same as the ones on your list in a)?

c Which do you think is the strangest festival? Tell your partner why.

FOOD FOR SPORT

1 Cheese rolling, Gloucestershire, England
Every May, hundreds of locals and international tourists run down a steep hill after a very fast double Gloucester cheese! As you can imagine there is a big risk of injury. The idea is to catch the cheese as it rolls down at speeds of up to 70km/h – something which is quite hard to do, due to both the speed and the fact that it starts before the runners!

2 La Tomatina, Buñol, Spain
On the last Wednesday in August, the people from this small town near Valencia throw overripe tomatoes at each other. The battle is part of a week-long festival and once the fun starts, tomatoes are thrown wildly at anything that moves. The fight then continues for an hour or two until a cannon is fired and everyone must calm down.

3 The Battle of the Oranges, Ivrea, Italy
Just before Lent every year residents of this north-west Italian town throw a different fruit at each other: oranges. People say that the oranges represent the head of an ancient duke who was beheaded in the town for his cruel ways. Of course, when it's cold the oranges are nearly frozen and they can really hurt.

4 The Night of the Radishes, Oaxaca, Mexico
In Oaxaca, Mexico the big Christmas celebration takes place on 23rd December, and they celebrate by making all kinds of things out of radishes – from small animals to scale models of carnivals. It is thought that the origin of this festival is connected to the Spanish missionaries who came to Mexico. Sadly, within 24 hours, the radishes start to rot, and it's all wasted!

5 Tunarama, Port Lincoln, South Australia
This event takes place during the January fish festival, and is a bit like the Olympic hammer event, but they throw a large tuna fish rather than a metal ball and chain. Anyone who wants to can have a go but the tuna must weigh between eight and 10 kilos. Former Olympic hammer thrower Sean Carlin holds the record: he threw his fish 37.23 metres.

exam expert

Writing

ISE Reading into Writing
➡ *See Writing file on pages 92-109.*

7 Now write an article (approximately 250 words) for a social studies publication:

i) summarising what is involved with the different festivals around the world **and**

ii) expressing your own feelings about whether customs like these are relevant in today's world.

ISE Portfolio/CW
➡ *See Writing file on pages 92-109.*

8 Choose one, or more, of these writing tasks.

Correspondence
Your Australian friend has asked you about national customs in your country. Write an email to this friend describing a national custom. Tell your friend what this custom is, how popular it is and why.

Factual writing *(ISE II 2009)*
'Young people are losing interest in traditional customs.' Write an article for a teenage magazine saying to what extent you agree or disagree with this statement. Support your point of view with an example of a particular National custom and say what young people's attitude towards this tradition is.

Creative/descriptive writing *(ISE II 2008)*
Write a description (approximately 250 words) of your favourite national customs for an English magazine. Describe the origin and history of these customs and say whether you think they will continue in the future.

Examiner: Which customs from your country might be difficult for people from another country?
Candidate: Well, timetables might be a problem, because people start work and school very early in the morning, at 7 a.m. usually.

UNIT 6
Pollution & recycling

A

B

C

D

Vocabulary

1a Look at the pictures above. What links are there between these items and the environment?

b Write Y (yes), N (no) or ? (not sure) about the place where you do your weekly shopping. Use your dictionary to help.

1. ☐ Is there a range of unbleached paper products?
2. ☐ Can you find bio-degradable washing products?
3. ☐ Are you encouraged to re-use shopping bags?
4. ☐ Are the bags they supply made from recycled plastic?
5. ☐ Do some of the products they sell come from renewable resources, e.g. wood from renewable forests?
6. ☐ Do they promote eco-friendly products with sales and discounts?

c Compare your results with a partner. Who is more aware of the products their supermarket sells? Whose supermarket is more environmentally-friendly?

d In pairs, discuss your opinions about the following.

1. Is **organic** food worth the extra money?
2. Do you do anything special to **save energy**?
3. What kinds of things can you **recycle** in your neighbourhood?
4. Do you buy **refillable** containers?

e Underline one word from each question in b) that refers to the environment, pollution or recycling. Now use these words to ask other questions.

Pollution & recycling

Reading

2a Read the article below and choose the best title for it.

A Congestion Charge has surprising benefits to health

B Congestion Charge less successful than planned

C Congestion Charge extending to other areas

A study has estimated that Londoners as a community are now living 1888 more years than they were before 2003. In 2003 the Mayor of London launched the Congestion Charge in central London, introducing an £8 daily charge for vehicles entering the city. In 2007, the zone was extended to include areas of west London.

The charge was introduced to reduce the amount of traffic in the city and to increase the funds available to improve public transport and facilities for cyclists and pedestrians. There are currently 5 types of vehicle exempt from the charge including: motorcycles, electric and hybrid cars and cars that use LPG gas or alternative fuels.

Initially, experts were not optimistic about the environmental impact of the charge. <u>Since</u> most of London's traffic is in outer London, where the zone does not apply, they estimated very low reductions in noise and air pollution.

<u>However</u>, recent studies show a 12% reduction in emissions. This reduction is thought to lead to the health benefits discovered and may also lead to reductions in heart attacks <u>as well as</u> child breathing problems. The reductions in emissions are <u>due to</u> the fact that there is less traffic and because traffic moves faster and faster moving vehicles produce less pollution.

b What is the significance of these numbers from the article?

1 1888   4 2007
2 5   5 12
3 8   6 2003

c With a partner, underline all the words you think are related to pollution in the article e.g. *air pollution*. How many words can you find?

d We use discourse markers to join ideas and sentences together. Which of the words below could replace the four discourse markers underlined in the text?

1 yet   4 as
2 in addition to   5 because of
3 nevertheless

e Rewrite each pair of sentences as one sentence using the words in brackets at the end. You'll have to do each one twice!

1 It was cold. They went for a swim. (*but despite this*) (*even though*)

2 There may be a reduction in heart attacks. There may be a reduction in breathing problems. (*in addition to*) (*and*)

3 There wasn't a recycling bin. They put it in the normal bin. (*since*) (*because*)

4 There is a shortage at the warehouse. There are no energy-saving light bulbs. (*because of*) (*due to*)

5 Organic vegetables in that store are expensive. He bought them anyway. (*however*) (*yet*)

41

UNIT 6

Writing

ISE Reading into Writing

→ See Writing file on pages 92-109.

3 Refer to the article about London's congestion charge. Write an article (approximately 250 words) for a school magazine:

i) summarising in your own words what the article says about the London congestion charge **and**

ii) suggesting reasons why a congestion charge should be introduced where you live.

Listening

4a Look at the photos. What kinds of pollution do they show? How do the different types of pollution make you feel?

b 🎧 27 Listen to the conversations about pollution and write the number of the conversation (1-5) on the correct photo. There is one extra photo which you will not need.

c 🎧 27 Listen again. Decide if the statements below are true (T) or false (F).

1 ☐ The woman in conversation 1 has asked the owners of the restaurant to tell their customers to make less noise.

2 ☐ The speakers in conversation 2 think that people need to understand more about the problem of water pollution.

3 ☐ The man in conversation 3 thinks that air pollution is worse in some places than others.

4 ☐ The woman in conversation 4 thinks that it's impossible to stop this type of pollution.

5 ☐ The man in conversation 5 thinks that the problem of this type of pollution can be helped by talking to people.

d What types of pollution annoy you? Discuss with a partner giving reasons why.

A

B

C

D

E

F

Pollution & recycling

Grammar focus

Simple passive

We use the simple passive when we don't know who did something or it is not important who did it.
object + *be* + verb (past participle)
Spanish **is spoken** in many countries around the world.

For the past, we just change the tense of the verb *be*.
Recycling glass **was first introduced** to our neighbourhood in 1995.

The simple passive is often used to describe how things are done.
First, **the paper is collected** from recycling bins.
Then **it is transported** to the factory for recycling...

If you want to show who did something you can do this with the word *by*.
The rubbish **is emptied by** the cleaner.

5a Look at the text on page 41. Can you find some examples of the passive?

b Change these sentences into the passive.
1. John kicked the ball.
2. The taxi picked her up from the shop.
3. The bus driver takes the boy to school.
4. On Tuesday the farmer delivers vegetables to the shop.

c Complete the description of how to recycle glass using the verbs in brackets.

How glass ¹............ **(*recycle*)**

Old bottles and jars ²............ (*throw*) into recycling bins. Then they ³............ (*collect*) from people's homes and ⁴............ (*take*) to a recycling plant. All the glass ⁵............ (*sort*) into colour groups and each one ⁶............ (*wash*) to remove any stains or left over food. Next the glass ⁷............ (*crush*) and ⁸............ (*melt*) then ⁹............ (*mould*) into new containers or ¹⁰............ (*turn into*) or other things. Finally the glass ¹¹............ (*send*) back to shops and factories so it ¹²............ (*can use*) again.

43

exam expert

Interactive phase

Taking control over the interaction

As part of the Interactive task, it is your responsibility to keep the interaction going. You have to take control. You'll have 4 minutes so take your time to explore the subject. One way of doing this is by asking questions.

6a Read the two prompts. With a partner, decide which questions belong to the prompt. Write A or B.

> **A** I'm thinking of studying at university in England, but I'm not sure what the best course would be.

> **B** I've been invited to a clean-up day by the local river but I'm not sure what to take with me.

1. ☐ Why England?
2. ☐ What would you normally use when you clean up your house?
3. ☐ Who invited you?
4. ☐ What kinds of things are you good at?
5. ☐ What would you do if you didn't study at university?
6. ☐ What exactly will you be doing on the day?

b 🎧 28 Work in pairs and follow these instructions.

- Listen to three prompts.
- Write two questions you could ask about each problem.
- Swap questions with another pair and correct any language problems.
- Get your questions back and check the corrections. Do you agree?

Topic phase

Concerns about your topic

7a 🎧 29 Listen to some people's concerns about the exam. Choose the appropriate suggestion (A-D) for each person. There is an extra one you do not need.

> **A** I don't think that will sound very natural. How about writing down notes and remembering them instead?

> **B** Have you tried thinking of other aspects of your topic? Perhaps there are other things that would make it more interesting.

> **C** How about taking something with you to help you remember things? Like a photo, a map, a ticket.

> **D** Why don't you choose something you know a lot about? Then I'm sure you'll be able to talk about it for five minutes.

b Write a list of the things you think might cause problems in your exam, then share your thoughts with a partner. Take it in turns to discuss your topics. Make some practical suggestions of what you could do.

exam expert

Conversation phase
Asking questions

8a In the Conversation phase for Grade 7, the examiner chooses two subjects from the list below (for ISE II there will be these plus another six.) Match the questions with the subjects.

- A Education
- B National customs
- C Village and city life
- D ~~Youth culture~~ Local Produce
- E Early memories
- F Pollution and recycling

1. ☐ What trends are popular with young people where you live?
2. ☐ Are there any laws in your city to reduce the amount of smog and car fumes in the air?
3. ☐ What is/was your favourite school subject?
4. ☐ Do you celebrate any festivals where you live?
5. ☐ If you moved to a big city like New York, what would you miss most?
6. ☐ What kinds of things do you remember from your childhood?

b In pairs, write down three questions you could ask for each of the subjects above.

c Your teacher will call out a subject. Student A (the examiner) should ask the questions s/he has for that subject. Student B (the candidate) should answer the questions, giving extra information. Keep asking questions until your teacher changes the subject. Change roles and start again.

Writing
ISE Portfolio/CW

➡ *See Writing file on pages 92-109.*

9 Choose one, or more, of these writing tasks.

Correspondence (*ISE II 2010*)

Write a letter to the editor of an international environmental publication explaining how your country's environment is being damaged by business activities. Express your feelings about the situation and emphasise the need for government action.

Factual writing (*ISE II 2011*)

Your area has been suffering from the effects of pollution. Write a report for an environmental committee explaining how the local landscape and lives of residents have been negatively affected by pollution. Make some suggestions to improve the situation.

Creative/descriptive writing (*ISE II 2007*)

If you were stranded on a desert island and could only bring three things, what would they be? Describe the three items and explain why you wouldn't want to be without them.

Trinity TAKE AWAY

Examiner: Tell me about what people do with their rubbish in your country.
Candidate: Well, most plastic, paper and glass rubbish **is recycled**. It **is collected** from people's houses every week and then it is taken to a recycling plant, where it **is made** into new products and **can be reused**.

Review Units 4-6

1 Choose the correct answer/s to the questions below.

1 Choose the correct word to complete the following sentence.

...is a place with trees, fields and very few houses around.

- **A** ☐ A town
- **B** ☐ A city
- **C** ☐ A village
- **D** ☐ The countryside

2 Which reply to the following statement is inappropriate?

I think that living in a town is better than living in the countryside.

- **A** ☐ I'm afraid I disagree completely.
- **B** ☐ I'm not sure that I agree with you.
- **C** ☐ I don't know about that.
- **D** ☐ I don't mind.

3 Which reply doesn't show full agreement with the following statement?

A city has a better atmosphere for children. There's more to do.

- **A** ☐ I agree completely.
- **B** ☐ I couldn't agree more.
- **C** ☐ I agree with you to a certain extent, but...
- **D** ☐ Yes, that's true.

4 Which modal verb cannot be used in the following sentence?

If she lived in the city, she .... have a better social life.

- **A** ☐ can
- **B** ☐ could
- **C** ☐ might
- **D** ☐ would

5 Choose the two possible options to complete the following sentence.

She's the woman .... lives on the second floor.

- **A** ☐ that
- **B** ☐ which
- **C** ☐ no relative pronoun
- **D** ☐ who

6 Which of the following phrases can be used to elicit further information from someone?

- **A** ☐ It would be interesting to hear what you have to say about...
- **B** ☐ If I were you, I would...
- **C** ☐ Talking about..., was there anything to do with... that you could tell me more about?
- **D** ☐ Tell me something about what... involves.

7 Which suggestions help people be 'greener'?

- **A** ☐ Use bio-degradable products.
- **B** ☐ Buy lots of fruit and vegetables.
- **C** ☐ Use renewable resources.
- **D** ☐ Don't buy products with unnecessary packaging.

8 Which reply to the following statement is incorrect?

I want to be more environmentally-friendly.

- **A** ☐ How about separating your rubbish for recycling?
- **B** ☐ Have you tried separate your rubbish for recycling?
- **C** ☐ Perhaps you could separate your rubbish for recycling?
- **D** ☐ What about separating your rubbish for recycling?

Review units 4-6

What do you remember about the Interactive phase of the exam?

2 Cross out the wrong words in the following statements so that they are true.

0 In the interactive phase, the examiner *takes/doesn't take* part.
1 The purpose of this phase *is to/is not to* take control of and maintain the conversation.
2 There is a focus on the *language functions/grammar and vocabulary* of the grade.
3 The examiner sets up the situation and then *he or she/the candidate* takes responsibility for keeping things going.
4 If you don't understand the situation, you *can/cannot* ask the examiner to repeat it.
5 Sometimes the situations involve role play. In this case, candidates are *free/not free* to be themselves.
6 If the candidate doesn't keep the conversation going, the examiner *will/will not* intervene and take control.
7 The candidate should *give yes-no answers/ask questions and comment* in response to the examiner.
8 The examiner's responses will be *shorter/longer* than the candidate's in this phase.
9 This phase should last around *four/five* minutes.
10 If the candidate doesn't take control, the phase will be shorter and the candidate *will not be/will be* marked very highly.

Exam tips – Interactive phase

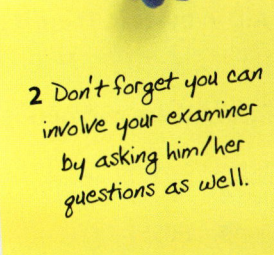

1 Remember that you need to be in control and not leave the examiner to do all the work. Be confident and take the lead.

2 Don't forget you can involve your examiner by asking him/her questions as well.

Units 4-6 Self-evaluation

Write Y (yes) or N (needs more practice) for each statement.

1 ☐ I can talk about village and city life.
2 ☐ I can talk about national customs.
3 ☐ I can talk about pollution and recycling.
4 ☐ I can use the second conditional correctly.
5 ☐ I can use relative clauses correctly.
6 ☐ I can use the passive correctly.

Now you write 'can do' statements like the ones above for the interactive and communicative skills you have practised in Units 4-6.

UNIT 7
National environmental concerns

Australia: Land of costly problems

There are numerous concerns for the environment in Australia: some new and accidental, others long-standing and the direct result of human activity, but all of them costly.

A ☐ include populations of mammals, such as rabbits and foxes; insects; birds; fungi and parasites; marine life, from fish to mussels and crabs and weeds, all of which were brought to Australia from other lands. These plants and animals pose a significant threat to Australia's bio-diversity because native species can become extinct or struggle to survive. Clearing weeds alone costs an estimated $13 billion a year.

B ☐ occurs when salt levels in the land increase. In some areas of Australia this is making once fertile land unsuitable for agriculture and animal grazing. In the past, native plants absorbed the salt in the dirt and salt levels in underground water were stable. However, with European agricultural practices and the removal of native plants, underground salt has washed into waterways and come to the ground's surface.

C ☐ levels have remained dangerous for over 50 years since British nuclear tests were conducted in the desert area of Maralinga. After numerous costly clean up operations, the site is still considered hazardous. Recently, the local Maralinga Tjarutja people were awarded $13.5 million in compensation.

D ☐ have occurred a few times in Australia's recent history including one in the Great Barrier Reef, one of Australia's most precious natural wonders. A coal ship was en route to China when it ran aground, damaging its fuel tank. Fortunately, the heavy fuel that escaped was broken up with chemicals, preventing an environmental catastrophe. Nevertheless the ship left a three kilometre scar on the reef, which may take 10-20 years to recover.

Reading

1a Look at the pictures of different environmental concerns. Match the words (1-5) to each picture (A-E).

1 ☐ Radiation
2 ☐ Introduced species
3 ☐ Oil spills
4 ☐ Litter
5 ☐ Soil salinity

b Match the words from the previous exercise (1-5) to paragraphs A-D in the text. There is one extra title.

c What is the significance of these numbers in the text?

1 a few   4 13
2 50   5 13.5
3 10-20   6 3

National environmental concerns

Vocabulary

2a Complete the table with the different forms of the words from the text.

Noun	Verb	Adjective
0 extinction	to become extinct	extinct
1 survival		
2	to invade	
3 population		
4 threat		
5	to prevent	
6	to recover	

b (30) Mark the word stress on each word as in the example. Can you pronounce them? Listen to the recording and check.

c Complete the sentences with a form of the word given.

1 Increasingly growing urban areas are threatening the .... of many animals and plants. (*survive*)
2 The complete .... of the plant's habitat mean that it became extinct. (*invade*)
3 Because some nature reserves are too small they actually divide .... of animals. (*populate*)
4 Controlling the numbers of whales that can be killed has enabled a .... in the numbers found. (*recover*)
5 The protest was about .... native species and national laws to protect them. (*threat*)
6 The best way to control introduced species is .... them from entering the area. (*prevention*)

Listening

3a In pairs, look at the photos and discuss the questions below.

1 What kind of environmental disaster do the pictures show?
2 Have you ever seen anything like this?
3 Has there ever been a similar event in your country?

b (31) Listen to the conversation and answer the questions below.

1 What is the name of the event?
2 What caused the accident?
3 How much fuel was spilled?

c Read this sentence from the audio, then answer the questions below.

'But really, if the cyclone had not hit, the accident wouldn't have happened.'

1 Did the cyclone hit?
2 Did the accident happen?

UNIT 7

Grammar focus

The third conditional

To talk about imaginary past events and their results we use the third conditional:
if + had (not) + past participle, + would (not) + have + past participle
If they had been more careful, the accident would not have happened.

In spoken and informal English we contract auxiliary verbs and negatives.
If the ship hadn't crashed, the oil wouldn't have spilled into the ocean.

We can change the order of the condition and the result. We don't use a comma here.
Would the accident have happened if they hadn't been so tired?

We often use the third conditional to talk about things we wish had happened in the past.
We wouldn't have used so many trees if we'd started recycling paper sooner.

We can use other modal verbs instead of would to talk about results.
If they'd known that an endangered species lived there, they might have saved it.
If we hadn't moved into their habitat, they could have survived.

4a Make sentences about the environmental disaster using clauses 1-5 and A-E. Sometimes there is more than one possibility.

1. ☐ If the cyclone hadn't hit,
2. ☐ If the containers hadn't moved,
3. ☐ If the other cargo had not been hit,
4. ☐ If less fuel had poured into the ocean,
5. ☐ If the clean-up groups had not worked so hard,

A the coast wouldn't have been polluted.
B the area would not have recovered so quickly.
C they wouldn't have hit the other cargo and made the spill.
D there wouldn't have been a spill.
E the containers wouldn't have moved.

b Complete the sentences using the verbs supplied.

1 If I'd studied harder, I .... better marks. (*get*)
2 If .... in the disabled car parking space, I wouldn't have got a fine. (*park*)
3 I would have done it better the first time if the instructions .... clearer. (*be*)
4 We .... to the beach if the weather had been better. (*go*)
5 Would you have started this course if you .... how hard it was? (*know*)
6 .... you .... to this city if someone had told you how expensive it was? (*move*)

c 🔊 32 Listen to four people talking about what happened to them. Write third conditional sentences about their situations.

1 ....
2 ....
3 ....
4 ....

National environmental concerns

Phonology

■ Contractions and weak forms in conditional sentences

5a (33) Underline the words in the following sentences that are contracted when spoken. Then listen and check your answers.

1   If I had known it was going to rain, I would have brought an umbrella.
2   She would have won the race if she had not fallen over at the end.
3   If we had not come early, we would not have got a place.

b (34) How are these words pronounced? Listen to the recording and repeat them.

1   I would have...
2   she would not have...
3   they had...
4   he had not...

c Now you practise. Read the story below and make third conditional sentences about it. Practise your sentences, making sure you get your contractions right.

Mark's Bad Day

Mark's alarm clock didn't work. He got up late. He didn't have breakfast. He was in a bad mood. He didn't catch his normal bus. He was late for an important meeting. His boss was angry. He got fired.

E.g. If Mark's alarm clock had worked, he wouldn't have got up late.

exam expert

Conversation phase

■ Exam practice

6a In the Conversation phase, the examiner might ask a question about national environmental concerns. Use vocabulary from the reading and the listening to write four questions about the environment.

E.g. What, for you, is the most important issue that **threatens** the **survival** of life on Earth?
Do you know of any animals that have become **extinct** in your country?

b Use your questions to practise the Conversation phase with a partner.

Writing

ISE Reading into Writing

➡ *See Writing file on pages 92-109.*

7 Refer to the article on page 48. Write an article (approximately 250 words) for a school magazine:

i)   summarising in your own words what the article says about concerns for the environment in Australia **and**

ii) discussing an environmental concern that is important to your country.

exam expert

Topic phase

Introduction to the phase

8a Complete the advice about what you should and shouldn't do in the Topic phase of the exam using the words in the box. There is one extra word.

> anticipate detail diagrams interested
> interaction five discussion

1 You should prepare a topic that you are .... in and know a lot about.
2 Don't prepare a speech. This phase should involve a .... about the topic between you and the examiner.
3 You should prepare enough material for the discussion to last for up to .... minutes.
4 You should use notes and/or ...., e.g. a 'mind map', to help you in the exam.
5 You should .... questions the examiner might ask you about your topic, and plan possible responses.
6 You should be prepared to explain what you've said in more .... if you're asked.

b Using information from this unit and following the advice above, prepare a topic about a national environmental concern.

c In pairs, take it in turns to present the information on your topic and lead a discussion about it.

d Decide with your partner how you think the discussions went. What do you feel you did well? What could be improved? Ask your teacher's opinion, too.

Interactive phase

Introduction to the phase

9a Decide if the statements below are true (T) or false (F), then rewrite the false statements.

1 ☐ It should last no longer than 6 minutes.
2 ☐ The candidate is responsible for keeping the conversation going.
3 ☐ This phase tests the candidate's ability to initiate conversations.
4 ☐ If the candidate does not keep the conversation going, the examiner will help them and take over.
5 ☐ The examiner should speak more than the candidate.
6 ☐ The candidate is free to take the conversation in any direction, as long as it is related to what the examiner has said.

b (35) Listen to this example dialogue from the Interactive phase.

c (36) Then listen to the same dialogue and when there is a pause, match a function (1-5) to what the candidate says (A-G). The candidate may use two functions, so you may need to use them more than once.

1 Making a suggestion or recommendation/giving advice
2 Comparing what the examiner says with something the candidate knows
3 Asking for information
4 Agreeing/Empathising/saying you are the same
5 Adding/giving information

d Here are some more expressions for the functions in c). Match the expressions (1-6) with the functions (A-F).

A Making a suggestion or recommendation/ giving advice
B Agreeing
C Comparing what the examiner says with something you know
D Adding/giving information
E Empathising/saying you are the same
F Asking for information

1 ☐ I know what you mean.
2 ☐ You should try the new restaurant.
3 ☐ What was it like?
4 ☐ It's much colder where I live.
5 ☐ It's a small place outside Rome where the king used to live.
6 ☐ I completely agree.

e Now work in pairs. Use the same prompt:

This is the first time I've ever been to this area and I have a free weekend.

Instead of asking a question first, use one of the other functions. Continue and try to use all the other functions from b) and c).

f How were your conversations different and the same as the example? How could you have improved the conversation?

Writing

ISE Portfolio/CW

➡ *See Writing file on pages 92-109.*

10 Choose one, or more, of these writing tasks.

Correspondence (ISE II 2008)

Write a letter to the environment agency in your country saying which environmental issue you think is the greatest cause for concern and proposing a national scheme to improve the situation.

Factual writing (ISE II 2009)

You would like to persuade more people in your area to protect the environment. Write a report for a community group making suggestions as to how everyone can make a contribution in their daily lives. Speculate about what will happen if people continue to damage the environment.

Creative/descriptive writing (ISE II 2008)

Write a description (true or imaginary) for a writing competition about a decision you made which completely changed your life. Speculate how your life would have been different if you had made a different decision.

Examiner: What mistakes do you think your country has made with regards to the environment?
Candidate: Well, that's a difficult question… I think **if they had invested more money in renewable energy, we wouldn't have such bad pollution** as we do today. We **would probably pay** less for electricity too!

UNIT 8

Personal values & ideals

Vocabulary

1a Number the items in the list according to the importance of these things in your life.
1 = most important, 6 = least important.

- [ ] family
- [ ] friends
- [ ] love
- [ ] money
- [ ] politics
- [ ] your home

b Work in pairs. Tell your partner about the order of your list, giving reasons.

Family is number 1 on my list. They help and support me. I couldn't manage without them.

2a Match values A–D with emails 1–4 on page 55 about how people live according to their values.

A compassion for people in need
B environmental principles
C ethical consumption
D ethical work
E bringing up children morally

b Work in pairs. Find out:

1 which of the values in a) your partner thinks are important.
2 what your partner does/has done/will do in the future to live according to these values.

Personal values & ideals

LIVING YOUR VALUES

Send us an email to tell us what you do. The most inspiring story wins 50 Euros for the charity of your choice!

1

Tony, London

I never take my kids to fast-food restaurants, **even though** they're cheap and appeal to children. I think the food they sell is bad for you, particularly for growing kids. **Something else** is that I try to buy Fair Trade products whenever I can, **for instance**, coffee and bananas. That way, I can be sure that the producer hasn't been exploited – that they get a fair price for their product.

2

Liz, Manchester

Although we've got a car, we try to use public transport whether we can. We're **also** careful about separating our rubbish for recycling. **Plus**, we reuse plastic carrier bags and buy products in packaging that can be recycled, **like** yogurts in glass jars, not plastic. I actually refuse to buy certain products, because the amount of packaging they come in is just ridiculous.

3

Carla, Madrid

One thing I do is to give money to people on the street – **in other words**, homeless people, people begging, people playing instruments to get money. They must be really desperate to be asking complete strangers for money. I just want to try and help a bit, although, realistically, giving them a few coins probably doesn't help that much – except to make me feel better!

4

Maria, New York

I once turned down a job **in spite of** the incredible salary on offer, because I found out that the company offering me the job was involved with the weapons industry. I thought about it a lot, and realised that I wouldn't feel comfortable making a living like that. It was hard to say no to all that money, **though**!

55

UNIT 8

Grammar focus

Linking words & phrases

3a Complete the table with the linking words and phrases in bold from the emails in exercise 2.

To introduce a point	To add another point	To give examples	To link contrasting points	To say something in another way
⁰...One thing...	¹.................... ².................... ³....................	⁴.................... ⁵....................	⁶.................... ⁷.................... ⁸.................... ⁹....................	¹⁰....................

Notice how the words and phrases to link contrasting points are used.

Even though Although Though	we've got a car, we try to use public transport whether we can.	
I never take my kids to fast-food restaurants,	**even though although though**	the food is cheap.
	It was hard to say no to all that money,	**though**.

I once turned down a job	**in spite of**	the incredible salary. (+ noun/noun clause) the fact that the salary on offer was incredible. (+ *the fact that* + verb clause) being offered an incredible salary. (+ verb+*ing* + noun clause)	
In spite of	the incredible salary on offer, the fact that the salary on offer was incredible, being offered an incredible salary,		I turned the job down.

b Complete the sentences with a word or phrase from a).

1 I hate discrimination, ..., when people are treated badly because they come from another country.

2 .... I don't have any religious beliefs myself, I think we should respect the beliefs of other people.

3 We recycle as much of our rubbish as possible. ...., we try to buy Fair Trade products.

4 Ethical consumption is a good idea. It can be quite difficult to put it into practice, ...

5 The people who are close to me are the most important thing in my life – ...., my family and friends.

6 .... I think that's really important is compassion for people in need. .... that's important to me is ethical work.

Personal values & ideals

Listening

4a 🎧37 Listen to the two conversations and decide which value each one relates to. Write the number of the conversation, 1 or 2, next to the value. There are two extra values in the list.

- A ☐ ethical consumption
- B ☐ ethical work
- C ☐ support of human rights
- D ☐ respect for animals

b 🎧37 Listen to conversation 1 again and put the sentences in the correct order.

- A ☐ But there are things you can do.
- B ☐ Or what about Amnesty International? You should join them. They do a really good job at promoting human rights.
- C ☐ You could join a protest group.

Persuading
Notice that when we want to **persuade** someone **to do something**, we usually:
- comment on the situation/problem
- make suggestions/give advice and justify it

c 🎧37 Listen to conversation 2 again and put the sentences in the correct order.

- A ☐ How could you enjoy a job like that?
- B ☐ I think it's a really bad idea.
- C ☐ Just think about what the company does.
- D ☐ Oh, but you can't!
- E ☐ You're not going to take the job, are you?

Discouraging
Notice that when we want to **discourage** someone **from doing something**, we usually:
- comment on the situation/problem
- dictate and justify the course of action

exam expert

Interactive phase

Exam practice

5 Work in pairs. One of you is Student A, the other Student B. Follow the instructions to practise persuading and discouraging in the Interactive phase.

Student A

Stage 1 You're the candidate. Listen to the examiner (Student B), explain the situation then persuade her/him to be more environmentally friendly.

Stage 2 You're the examiner. Explain the following situation to the candidate and respond to her/his attempts to persuade you:
- *You often pass people in need on the street, but you never give them money.*

Stage 3 Repeat Stage 1, but this time **discourage** the examiner from eating at fast food restaurants.

Stage 4 Repeat Stage 2, but this time, but this time with the following situation:
- *You're thinking about joining the army as a career.*

Stage 5 Decide with Student B what went well in the conversations and what you could improve.

Student B

Stage 1 You're the examiner. Explain the following situation to the candidate (Student A) and respond to her/his attempts to **persuade** you to change.
- *You don't recycle any of your household rubbish because you think it's too much effort.*

Stage 2 You're the candidate. Explain the following situation to the candidate, then **persuade** her/him to be more generous to people in need.

Stage 3 Repeat Stage 1, but this time with the following situation:
- *You love fast food and eat at fast food restaurants at least three times a week.*

Stage 4 Repeat Stage 2, but this time **discourage** the examiner from joining the army as a career.

Stage 5 Decide with Student A what went well in the conversations and what you could improve.

UNIT 8

Reading

6a Work in pairs. Make a list of charities that you know of and note what they do.

b Read the text about a charity called VSO and answer these questions.

1. Was VSO on your list in a)?
2. What does VSO do?

c Read the text again. Find and underline at least five reasons for volunteering with VSO. Compare your reasons with a partner.

d Work with a partner. Ask and answer these questions.

1. What do you think would be the best thing about being a volunteer with VSO?
2. What do you think a volunteer might find difficult?
3. Would you like to volunteer with VSO? Why/why not?

Looking for a change in your life? Why not volunteer overseas with VSO – the world's leading independent international development organisation that works through volunteers to fight poverty in developing countries. You'll make a real difference – not only to your life, but to the lives of some of the world's poorest people.

We work on long-term, sustainable solutions – we send volunteers rather than money. We have hundreds of volunteers working abroad in rewarding roles in over 40 countries. Volunteering gives them invaluable professional experience, a wealth of memories, and a whole new perspective on life. Most people join us because they want to 'give something back' and find they get much more in return.

Volunteering is a hands-on way of building a fairer world, one that allows you to get out of your usual routine and experience a culture that's often different from your own. Every year, thousands of professionals from

a wide range of backgrounds contact us. Most have a strong desire to experience giving something back in another part of the world and to embark on a fresh challenge. Right now, over 1,500 volunteers are working in highly-valued roles, helping to tackle the root causes of poverty.

International volunteering is at the heart of our contribution to development. We work with our overseas partners to bring together people from different cultures and backgrounds, enabling them to share skills and learning. These partnerships lead to new ways of achieving shared goals, and have a greater impact than simply transferring material resources.

If you want to do something practical to improve life for the poorest people in the world, volunteering with us could just be the answer.

exam expert

Writing
ISE Reading into Writing

→ *See Writing file on pages 92-109.*

7 Write an article (approximately 250 words) for a university website:

   i) summarising in your own words the work of VSO **and**

   ii) suggesting reasons why students should consider volunteering with the organisation.

Topic phase
■ Choosing a topic

8a Work in pairs. Make a list of all the topics you could talk about in the exam.

b Now ask each other these questions about the topics on your list.

   1 Is this topic too complicated, too technical or too difficult for me?

   2 Am I really interested in this topic?

   3 Can I make this topic interesting for myself and the examiner?

   4 Do I really know enough about this topic?

   5 Can I find out more about this topic?

c Using your answers from b), reject any unsuitable topics and make a shortlist of three possible topics.

d Choose one of the topics from your shortlist in c). Prepare a presentation on this topic by making a mind map and making notes.

e Work in pairs. Take it in turns to lead a discussion about your chosen topic and see how long you can keep the discussion going.

f Decide how you think the discussions went. What do you feel you did well? What could be improved? Ask your teacher's opinion, too.

Writing
ISE Portfolio/CW

→ *See Writing file on pages 92-109.*

9 Choose one, or more, of these writing tasks.

Correspondence (ISE II 2011)

Your Irish friend has decided to work as a volunteer for a charity in a developing country. Write him a letter highlighting the advantages and disadvantages of his decision and saying how you feel about it. Ask for more information about the charity.

Factual writing (ISE II 2011)

Write a review for a culture magazine of a film which has influenced your personal values. Summarise the plot and give your opinion on the actors' performances. Explain how the film has influenced the person you are today.

Creative/descriptive writing (ISE II 2011)

Write a story for a writing competition about a lazy school boy who eventually became a successful businessman. Describe how he used to behave, what happened to change him and the effect it had on his life.

Examiner: What are the most important values for you? Things you really believe in?
Candidate: Well, I've got strong environmental principles. I really believe that we all need to do as much as we can to help protect the environment, for instance, by recycling our rubbish.

UNIT 9
Public figures

A B C D E F

Listening

1a What type of public figures are shown in the pictures? Match the type (1-6) to the pictures (A-F). Can you name the people?

1. ☐ artist
2. ☐ actor
3. ☐ singer
4. ☐ sports person
5. ☐ politician
6. ☐ religious leader

b (38) Listen to four speakers, what types of public figures are they? Choose from the list 1-6 from the previous exercise.

Vocabulary

2a (38) Match the words to make expressions. They are all from the recording in exercise 1b). Listen again to check.

1. ☐ the price
2. ☐ in front of
3. ☐ to escape
4. ☐ personal
5. ☐ to get someone's
6. ☐ to be

A. the camera
B. life
C. of fame
D. the attention
E. under pressure
F. autograph

b Complete the sentences below with an expression or word from the exercise above.

1. I really don't see what my .... has to do with my job as a politician.
2. I waited for five hours outside the stage door to .... He wrote it on my T-shirt.
3. I'm not so sure I like all this fame. I feel I'm .... to perform all the time.
4. Nothing I do will ever .... of the media. They watch everything I do.
5. I wasn't very comfortable .... at first. But now I'm used to it.
6. I can't do anything without it appearing in the newspaper. I guess it's ....

c Look at the recording script for track 38. Find other words or expressions that might be useful for describing public figures, the work they do and how they might feel.

Public figures

Grammar focus

Past Perfect

To talk about a past event that happened before another past event, we use the Past Perfect:
subject + *had* (*not*) + past participle

In spoken English we often contract the auxiliary verb.
subject + *'d* (*hadn't*) + past participle
I hadn't realised Robbie was about my height before I met him. He looks taller on TV.

We often use the adverb *already* with perfect tenses like the Past Perfect.
subject + *had* (*not*) + *already* + past participle
I went to her hotel to see her. Unfortunately, she'd already left by the time I got there.

We often use the Past Perfect with the Past Simple to show the order of events. We can use many different time conjunctions to join the events and emphasise the timing.
By the time they arrived in Italy, they had travelled to twenty countries on their world tour.

The passive is formed like this: subject + *had* (*not*) + *been* + past participle.
After the votes had been counted, the Prime Minister announced that he had lost the election.

3a Complete these sentences with the Past Perfect of the verb supplied.

1. When did you realise you .... the money? (*win*)
2. I can't believe you .... of him before. He's so famous in my country. (*hear*)
3. They didn't get married until they .... enough money to build a house. (*save*)
4. After he .... for 45 minutes he gave up and went home. (*wait*)
5. No, it was my first time in Sicily. Even though I'm from Italy, I .... there. (*be*)
6. After she .... all she could, she went out into the cold snow. (*eat*)
7. She only told me after I .... I would leave her if she didn't tell me the truth. (*threaten*)
8. The plane .... when I got there, so I got to see them. (*take off*)

b Use the verbs supplied to complete the text with the Past Simple or the Past Perfect. Be careful: some of the verbs require a passive.

Toni Morrison [1]................... (*born*) on 18 February 1931 in Ohio, USA. By the time her first novel [2]................... (*publish*) she [3]................... (*marry and divorce*), [4]................... (*give birth*) to two sons and [5]................... (*teach*) in numerous universities in the States.
In 1987 Morrison [6]................... (*won*) the Pulitzer Prize for her novel *Beloved*. After winning the prize she [7]................... (*appoint*) to a chair at Princeton University, the first black woman writer to hold such a position at an Ivy league university. Morrison's success continued when she [8]................... (*win*) a Nobel Prize for Literature in 1993 after she [9]................... (*write*) her work *Jazz*.

UNIT 9

c When we are telling a story, especially one that progresses through time, or talking about people's lives, we use different time references. Mark all the time references in the text about Toni Morrison.

d Choose a time reference to complete the sentences. In one sentence more than one answer is possible.

1 .... I hated watching TV in England. But slowly I learned to enjoy it .... I had been there a few months.
   A At the beginning, after
   B At the beginning, before
   C One day, after

2 I never used to like the radio. But .... I've been listening on the drive to work. I really enjoy it.
   A at the time
   B recently
   C when

3 We're only going to be here .... So that doesn't give you much time. Hurry up!
   A at the time
   B after a while
   C for a while

4 Now, ... you start complaining about my cooking, I've done the best I can!
   A before
   B after
   C at the time

5 I grew up in the 1920s. We didn't have electricity .... We had to heat water on a fire.
   A at that time
   B at the time
   C recently

6 I don't know when we'll go to a Robbie Williams concert. But I promise you, ... we'll go.
   A at the beginning
   B one day
   C after

Phonology

Intonation in questions

6a Listen. Does the intonation go up or down at the end of each question?

1 Do you like playing football?
2 Where do you play?
3 You've been playing for a long time, haven't you?
4 You aren't going to stop playing, are you?

b Listen to the recording. Write A if the people are checking/asking a question or B if they are confirming information.

1 ☐ There are five members of Take That, aren't there?
2 ☐ You go down here to get to the stage door, don't you?
3 ☐ You'd like to study in Canada one day, wouldn't you?
4 ☐ They don't like watching scary films, do they?

Which intonation do you use for each meaning?

c Complete the following questions with a tag. In pairs, practise saying them using different intonation. Decide if your partner is asking a question or confirming information.

1 You can swim, ...?
2 He has got two brothers, ...?
3 They come to class on scooters, ...?
4 We're going to pass our exam, ...?

exam expert

Topic phase

Using mind maps

You can use mind maps to make notes about your topic. You can take a mind map in the exam to help you remember what you want to talk about and for the examiner to refer to.

7a 🎧 Francesca is preparing a topic about the singer Robbie Williams using a recording of a radio programme. Listen to the excerpts and complete her notes on the mind map.

October 2002: contract for ⁵ .... with EMI.
August 2003: biggest ⁶ .... in the UK.
September 2004: official ⁷ .... released.
2010 re-joined his original group Take That.

Started in a band called ¹ ....
No one expected him to be a ² .... at first.
Album, ³ '.............. thru a lens' became a big hit after ⁴ .... weeks in the charts.

I love his smile.
I admire his courage and determination to keep trying.
I love to listen to his music and sing along.

ROBBIE WILLIAMS

Member of fan club since 2003
Receive online newsletters
Read news on tours, new songs, media appearances
Download songs

'Angels'
'Come undone'
'Something Stupid' – with Nicole Kidman

b The mind map above contains too much information to take into the exam. Complete the mind map that Francesca will use in the exam. What discussion points would you add to the empty boxes?

c Remember you can take an object, photo or picture, etc. into the exam to help you. What could Francesca take with her? Make a list and compare it with a partner.

d Find out about a famous person and make notes about her/him. Redraft the notes you made into a concise mind map. In pairs, take it in turns to present the information and lead a discussion about your famous person.

e Decide with your partner how you think the discussions went. What do you feel you did well? What could be improved? Ask your teacher's opinion, too.

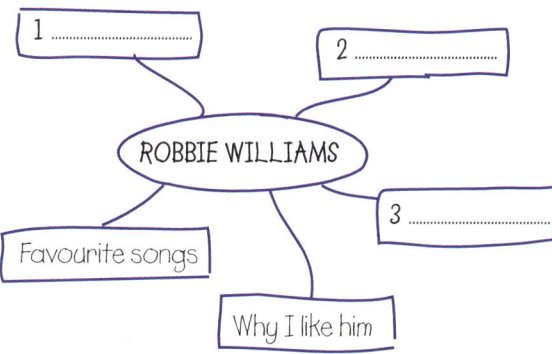

63

exam expert

Interactive phase

■ Keeping the conversation going

8a You will need to keep the conversation going in the Interactive task yourself. A good way of doing this is by asking questions. Varying the ways you ask questions will make the conversation more interesting.

Match these three different questions (1-3) to their type (A-C).

1 ☐ You're an actor, aren't you?
2 ☐ Are you English?
3 ☐ When were you born?

A yes/no questions
B information questions
C tag questions

Which types of questions do you think will be most useful in the Interactive phase?

b Reorder the words to make interview questions for a famous person.

1 you/Spain/born/were/in/?
2 you/how/famous/become/did/?
3 aren't/40/you're/you/over/?
4 grow/where/you/up/did/?
5 university/did/go/you/to/?
6 work/don't/you/too/you/music/in/?
7 you/celebrity/like/do/being/TV/a/?
8 Chinese/speak/you/can't/can/you/?
9 earn/film/per/how/do/much/you/?
10 your/isn't/photo/in/is/the/ paper/the/time/all/it/?

c Match the questions from b) with their type (A, B or C) from a).

d The Interactive task starts with a prompt from the examiner. Your teacher will read a prompt. Write down three questions, one for each question type in a), that you could ask about the prompt.

e Practise now with your partner. Using the prompts the teacher reads and the questions you wrote, practise a few of the prompts together. How long can you keep talking together?

exam expert

Conversation phase

Responding appropriately

9a 🎧 42 In the Conversation phase the examiner will check how well you understand by how you respond. Listen to the responses to these questions. Why are they inappropriate?

1 What things would you miss about ordinary life if you were a celebrity?
2 Who are the most famous people where you live?
3 What do you think it would be like to be famous?

b Discuss these questions in groups and compare your answers. Do you have the same opinion?

1 Name some famous people from your country. Who appears in the media the most?
2 Do public figures have a right to keep their personal life private?
3 The media say they have the right to report about people's private lives if it is in the 'public interest'. What kinds of things should and should not be reported in your opinion?

Writing

ISE Portfolio/CW

➡ *See Writing file on pages 92-109.*

10 Choose one, or more, of these writing tasks.

Correspondence (*ISE II 2011*)

Your local council is planning to erect a statue of a well-known public figure in your area. Write a letter to the council explaining why you disagree with the person suggested and persuading them to reconsider the plan. Recommend a more suitable public figure for the statue.

Factual writing (*ISE II 2008*)

The Principal of your school or college would like to invite a public figure to come and give a speech to inspire the students. Write a report for the principal proposing two public figures that could be invited and recommending which one you think would be best.

Creative/descriptive writing (*ISE II 2009*)

Imagine you went on a long bus journey and sat next to Lou Star, a popular musician from the 1960s who is no longer famous. Write a description for a website called 'www.forgotten-stars.com' saying what he told you about his life and career. Describe his feelings about his life then and now.

Examiner: Have you ever met anyone famous?
Candidate: Well, I didn't really meet them but I did see someone famous near where I live. **I'd just finished** at the gym and I was walking home when I saw Pink walking in the street.

Review Units 7-9

1 **Join the two clauses (1-6 and A-F) together to make correct sentences.**

1 ☐ When I arrived at the airport
2 ☐ We got a ticket for the plane
3 ☐ If my sister hadn't lent us her car,
4 ☐ They had cancelled the appointment
5 ☐ I'd have missed the meeting
6 ☐ Despite the fact that there were so many people in the queue

A in spite of arriving at the airport only one hour before it left.
B we'd have come by bus.
C the plane had already left.
D if the plane hadn't arrived on time.
E there were plenty of empty seats in the plane.
F the day before we were due to meet.

2 **Complete the sentences using the verbs in brackets based on the events below.**

Aiden didn't set his alarm last night. He woke up late and missed his train. He, therefore, arrived at work late and unfortunately missed an important meeting with a client. Because of that, he lost the account with the client and his boss fired him. Poor Aiden!

1 If Aiden .... (set) his alarm, he .... (wake up) late.
2 If he .... (wake up) on time, he .... (miss) his train.
3 He .... (arrive) at work late if he .... (catch) his train.
4 He .... (be) at the meeting if he .... (arrive) at work late.
5 If he .... (miss) the meeting, he .... (loose) the account.
6 If he .... (win) the account, he .... (be) unemployed.

Poor Aiden!

3 **Complete the sentences using the words at the end in brackets. Be careful, the words at the end are in the wrong form and need to be changed.**

1 Twenty-five percent of the .... of London are from a non-British background. (*populate*)
2 Many animals may become .... if we don't act to save their habitat. (*extinction*)
3 It must be difficult to be an overnight super star and have to deal with being .... (*fame*)
4 They were trapped in the cave without food for ages. They were lucky to .... (*survival*)
5 It is better to work with people to .... disease rather than treat them after they have got it. (*prevention*)
6 Now that he has appeared on TV a few times, he is starting to get .... wherever he goes. (*recognise*)
7 Which animals and plants are under .... in your country? (*threatened*)
8 If I was famous, I would not want my .... life to be talked about in the newspaper. (*person*)
9 It takes many years for an environment to .... after an oil spill. (*recovery*)
10 A famous person like the Pope or a president can never .... the attention of the press. (*escaping*)

66

Review units 7-9

What do you remember about the Conversation phase of the exam?

4 Complete this summary with the words provided below.

choose   consists   demonstrating   maintain   participate   prepared   put forward   take

The purpose of this part of the exam is to provide candidates the opportunity to ¹.................. in a genuine exchange of information, ideas and opinions while ².................. their ability to use the language from the grade.

It ³.................. of a discussion of two of the subject areas for the grade. Although the examiner will only ⁴.................. two, candidates need to be ⁵.................. to speak about all of them.

Candidates will be expected to:

⁶.................. more responsibility for the content of the conversation;

⁷.................. their ideas and opinions as well as information;

⁸.................. the flow; demonstrate a range of language and vocabulary.

Exam tips – Conversation phase

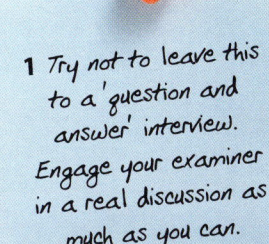

1 Try not to leave this to a 'question and answer' interview. Engage your examiner in a real discussion as much as you can.

2 The conversation will be about a topic related to the subject areas. Try to extend your vocabulary in these areas to help you be able to talk widely and more accurately.

Units 7-9 Self-evaluation

Write Y (yes) or N (needs more practice) for each statement.

1 ☐ I can talk about national environmental concerns.

2 ☐ I can talk about personal values and ideals.

3 ☐ I can talk about public figures.

4 ☐ I can talk about imaginary past events and their results using the third conditional.

5 ☐ I can use linking expressions and cohesive devices correctly.

6 ☐ I can talk about past events that happened before other past events using the Past Perfect.

Now you write 'can do' statements like the ones above for the interactive and communicative skills you have practised in Units 7-9.

GRADE 8

UNIT **10**

Society & living standards

business conditions
climate/sunshine
cultural resources
education
environmental issues
health care
housing
human rights
political and economic stability
public transport
quality of architecture
recreation facilities
safety/crime
tolerance
traffic congestion
water availability and drinkability

Vocabulary

1a Work with a partner. Look at the list of possible criteria for judging living standards and choose the ten most important ones in your opinion.

b For each criterion you chose in a), decide with your partner how the place where you live rates on a scale of 1-10, with 10 as the most positive, 1 as the most negative.

I think the traffic congestion in this city is terrible – let's give it one out of ten.

Well, the climate is pretty good here – there's lots of sunshine! Shall we say nine out of ten for that?

68

Society & living standards

Reading

2a Read the text and answer these questions.

1. Which of the criteria from exercise 1 are mentioned?
2. Are any additional criteria mentioned?

b Work with a partner and answer these questions.

1. Are there any criteria mentioned in the text that you don't think are good measures of living standards? Explain why.
2. Is the place where you live high on the list in the surveys? Why/Why not?

Writing

ISE Reading into Writing

➡ *See Writing file on pages 92-109.*

3 Read the text again and then, in your own words, write a report (approximately 250 words) for a sociology group:

i) explaining how living standards surveys are measured in the surveys **and**

ii) expressing your own feelings about the criteria used for measuring living standards in relation to the place where you live.

Mercer's Quality of Living Survey

This annual survey compares 221 cities based on 39 criteria, including safety, education, hygiene, health care, culture, environment, recreation, political-economic stability and public transportation.

In the 2010 list of cities, Europe is at the top of the list, with first place going to Vienna, Austria, second to Zürich and third to Geneva, both cities in Switzerland. There are several entries from Canada, Australia and New Zealand. Switzerland and Germany both have three cities in the top ten. The first entries from other countries are Singapore at 28, Honolulu, USA at 31, and Tokyo, Japan at 40. Compared to lists for previous years, cities in South Asia (mainly India), East Asia (mainly China), the Middle East and Eastern Europe are clearly on the rise.

2010's ranking also identifies the cities with the best environmental conditions, based on water availability and drinkability, waste removal, quality of sewage systems, air pollution and traffic congestion. Calgary, Canada, is at the top of this index.

Economist Intelligence Unit survey

This 'livability' survey shows cities in Canada, Australia, Austria, Finland and New Zealand as the ideal destinations

Vienna

Melbourne

thanks to a widespread availability of goods and services, low personal risk and an effective infrastructure. The 2010 report considers Vancouver, Canada to be the most livable city in the world, with Vienna taking second place, followed by Melbourne, Australia. The survey said that, in the current global political climate, it was no surprise that the most desirable destinations were those with a lower threat of terrorism.

The Economist survey has been criticised, however, and the US newspaper the New York Times reported that 'The Economist clearly equates livability with speaking English.'

The Most Liveable Cities Index

The lifestyle magazine Monocle publishes an annual non-scientific survey of liveable cities, in which it presents 25 top places for quality of life. Important criteria in this survey are safety/crime, international connectivity, climate/sunshine, quality of architecture, public transportation, tolerance, environmental issues and access to nature, urban design, business conditions, pro-active policy developments and medical care. The winning city in 2010 was Vancouver, Canada, followed by Vienna in second place and Melbourne, Australia, in third place.

UNIT 10

Reported speech

1 When we report what someone said, we often change the tenses of the verbs:
*The survey said that, 'In the current global climate, it **is** no surprise that the most desirable destinations **are** those with a lower threat of terrorism.'*
→ *The survey **said** that... it **was** no surprise that the most desirable destinations **were** those...*

2 If things are still true when we report them, the tenses can either change or stay the same:
*The US newspaper The New York times reported that 'The Economist clearly **equates** livability with speaking English.'*
→ *The US newspaper The New York times reported that The Economist clearly **equates/equated** livability...*

3 In reported questions, *ask*, not *say*, is used as the reporting verb, and the word order is different:
'What are living standards like in your country, Karen?'
→ *She **asked** her/Karen what living standards were like in her country.*

4 When we are reporting a question without a question word (*how/why/who* etc.), we use *if* or *whether*.
'Do you think healthcare or education is more important?'
→ *She **asked** me **whether** I thought healthcare or education **are/were** more important.*

5 In reported orders, requests and suggestions we often use reporting verb + personal direct object + infinitive with *to*:
'Don't spend all your money on sweets.'
  Mum **told me not to spend** all my money on sweets.
'Please give me your Portfolio work next week.'
→ *The teacher **asked us to give** her our Portfolio work next week.*

6 We use *tell* + personal direct object to specify who we tell. We use *say* without a personal object:
*The teacher **told us** that we had done well.*
→ *The teacher **said** that we had done well.*
not ~~The teacher said us~~.

4a Use the information above to rewrite these statements and questions in reported speech.

1 John said, 'I'm really short of money this month.'
2 Jenny said, 'I've been saving money for a holiday.'
3 The Prime Minister said, 'Inflation could increase again this month.'
4 'Have living standards improved in this country in the last few years?' (*The examiner...*)
5 'Do you want tea or coffee?' (*He...*)
6 'Who are you going on holiday with?' (*She...*)

b Rewrite these orders, requests and suggestions in reported speech.

1 'Hurry up!' (*She told me...*)
2 'Please don't do that.' (*He...*)
3 'You should spend more time on your homework.' (*The teacher...*)
4 'Stop shouting!' (*He...*)

Society & living standards

5a Match the reporting verbs (A-H) with their definitions (1-8).

A advise
B complain
C discuss
D explain
E promise
F warn
G wonder
H report

1. ☐ to give more information, or reasons, about something
2. ☐ to tell someone what you think she/he should do
3. ☐ to say that you will definitely do, or not do, something
4. ☐ to say that you do not like, or are unhappy with, something
5. ☐ to give information about something
6. ☐ to tell someone that something bad may happen
7. ☐ to talk about something
8. ☐ to ask yourself something

b Complete the following sentences with a reporting verb from a).

1. He .... that he had too much work to do.
2. I .... with a friend what to do about the problem.
3. My dentist .... me to brush my teeth after every meal.
4. She .... not to arrive late this time.
5. The teacher .... that the exam was to test our reading skills in English.
6. The teacher .... us that if we didn't study more, we wouldn't pass the exam.
7. The newspaper .... what the prime minister said in her speech yesterday.
8. I .... whether we should go on holiday in July or August?

6a Write five sentences giving your opinion about society and living standards where you live.

E.g. Recreation facilities could be improved a lot – for instance, there are no public swimming pools in my area.

b Work in pairs. Find out what your partner put in their list in a).

c Change partners. Report what your partner from b) said about society and living standards.

E.g. Luis said that he thought that healthcare here is quite good.

He complained about public transport. He said that we need a better bus network.

Phonology

Connected speech

7a 🎧 43 Listen to each of the words in the list and practice saying them.

> Mum told me not to spend all my money on sweets

b 🎧 44 Now listen to the same words together in a sentence. The letters where the final sound in a word is lost are underlined. The letters where the last sound of a word runs into the next word are circled.

Mum tol<u>d</u> me no<u>t</u> t<u>o</u> spen(d all my money on) sweets.

UNIT 10

c 🎧45 Work with a partner. Decide where sounds are lost and where they run into the next word in these sentences. Show this by underlining and circling, as in the example in b). Listen to check.

1 She asked me whether I would prefer to live in New York or Honolulu.
2 The teacher asked us to give her our opinions about living standards in our country.
3 He advised me to wait until I was older to apply for the volunteer job.
4 They warned us that there would be serious problems if we didn't do something soon.
5 I wonder what the government is doing to improve living conditions in this country.

d Take it in turns to listen to your partner saying the sentences from c).

> It doesn't matter if you don't use these features of connected speech when you speak English, but you need to be familiar with how they change the sounds of words to be able to understand native speakers more easily.

e Now think of a recent conversation you had with someone in your family or a friend. Report it to your partner.

exam expert

Interactive, Conversation and Topic phases

■ Maintaining the interaction

8a Complete the information about how to keep a conversation going using the words and phrases in the box.

> ask   real   show   showing

A useful way of keeping a conversation going is to ¹................. interest in what the other person is saying. To do this you can ²................. **a reply question**, then **a follow-up question**.

Examiner: Since the introduction of the Euro I think life has become more expensive.

Candidate: Do you? What sort of things have you noticed changing?

The reply 'Do you?' is a way of ³................. interest, not a ⁴................. question – this comes with the follow-up question, 'What sort of things have you noticed changing?'

b 🎧46 Listen to the statements and choose a reply question (A–C) that matches.

1 A ☐ Have you?   C ☐ Do you?
  B ☐ Can she?
2 A ☐ Can we?   C ☐ Do we?
  B ☐ Does he?
3 A ☐ Has it?   C ☐ Were they?
  B ☐ Was it?
4 A ☐ Can they?   C ☐ Can you?
  B ☐ Could you?
5 A ☐ Will he?   C ☐ Won't he?
  B ☐ Would she?

c 🎧47 Now listen to four different statements. Write two possible reply questions for each.

1 *Do you?/Are they?*

d 🎧47 Listen to the statements from c) again and write follow-up questions to ask after each reply question.

1 *I think children are less respectful these days. Do you? What makes you say that?*

exam expert

e Write a short statement about society and living standards. It should be something that someone can react to, similar to the statements you heard in b) and c).

f Work in pairs. One of you is Student A, the other Student B. Follow the instructions.

Student A

Stage 1 You're the examiner, Student B is the candidate. Share your statement about living standards from e) with the candidate and respond to their questions.

Stage 2 You're the candidate, Student B is the examiner. Respond to the examiner's statement with reply and follow-up questions to keep the conversation going (for four minutes).

Student B

Stage 1 You're the candidate, Student A is the examiner. Respond to the examiner's statement with reply and follow-up questions to keep the conversation going (for four minutes).

Stage 2 You're the examiner, Student A is the candidate. Share your statement about living standards from e) with the candidate and respond to their questions.

Writing

ISE Portfolio/CW

➡ *See Writing file on pages 92–109.*

9 Choose one, or more, of these writing tasks.

Correspondence (ISE II 2009)

You are living and working as a volunteer for an international charity in a developing country. Write a letter to a close friend explaining how your living standards have changed and saying how you have been feeling.

Factual writing (ISE II 2011)

You have been investigating living standards in your country. Write a report for a government committee saying what factors affect people's living standards and whether or not they have improved in the last 5 years. Suggest what could be done to ensure a good standard of living for all.

Creative/descriptive writing

Write a description of your ideal society for an online forum for young people. Describe how the society is organised, giving details of the living standards that make it ideal.

Examiner: Do you think living standards are good where you live?
Candidate: Well, I don't think they're too bad, although it depends how you judge living standards, I suppose. It's quite a safe place to live, and it's very clean, and there are good schools and universities. But traffic's a problem, and it's difficult for young people to find work – and the weather could be better!

GRADE 8

UNIT 11

The world of work

A

B

C

D

E

F

G

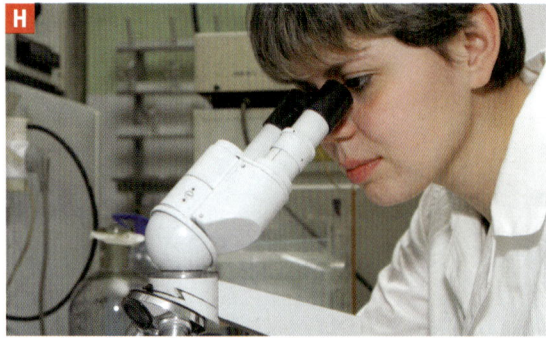
H

Vocabulary

1a Work with a partner. Which jobs do the photos show?

I think the woman in A is an engineer.

b With your partner, ask and answer the questions.

1. What does each job in a) involve exactly?
2. Which job in a) do you think is the hardest? Give reasons.
3. Which of the jobs in a) would you like to do? Give reasons.
4. Are there any jobs in a) that you wouldn't like to do? Explain why.
5. What would your dream job be, i.e. What would you do if you could choose any job?

E.g. Being an engineer can involve designing things, building things.

The world of work

■ **Expressing feelings about work**

2a Read the blog posts about people's jobs. Tick (✓) the box if they like their job, put a cross (✗) if they dislike it.

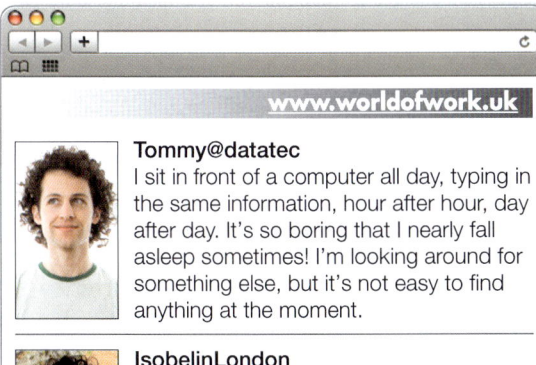

www.worldofwork.uk

Tommy@datatec
I sit in front of a computer all day, typing in the same information, hour after hour, day after day. It's so boring that I nearly fall asleep sometimes! I'm looking around for something else, but it's not easy to find anything at the moment.

IsobelinLondon
I'd say my job is challenging. There's a lot I need to learn, and it's stressful at times, like when I have to deal with a difficult client, or when we've got deadlines to meet. But, overall, I enjoy it – and I'm certainly never bored!

jonManchester88
I never know what's going to happen next in my job – every day is different, which makes it quite exciting. I work really hard, though. I often start the day with breakfast meetings, then all day I have to be creative, thinking up new ideas. The downside is that the job uses up all my energy – I don't really do anything in my free time because I'm too tired.

sara@schooldays
My job is very demanding. Being responsible for thirty six-year-old children is hard work! But it's also very rewarding – when you see that they're really learning, it's wonderful!

tillyAuckland87
I used to enjoy my job. The people I work with are nice, my boss is OK. The problem is, I've realised I'm just not interested in the products we produce. I just don't feel motivated by my work anymore.

b Underline the words and phrases in the blog posts used to express positive and negative feelings about work.

Function focus
Expressing feelings about work
Positive feelings
I **enjoy** *it.*   *I'm* never **bored**.
...which **makes** *it quite* **exciting**.   *...it's* also very **rewarding**.   *...it's* **wonderful**!
Negative feelings
It's so **boring**.   *...and it's* **stressful** *at times.*
...the job uses up all my energy.
It's **hard work**!
I just **don't feel motivated by** *my work.*
Positive or negative feelings
I'd say my job is **challenging**.
My job is very **demanding**.

Phonology

3a 🔊48 Listen to the two phrases and underline the stressed words/syllables in each one.

1 It's wonderful!
2 It's quite stressful.

b 🔊48 Listen again. Which phrase has the most changes in intonation, 1 or 2?

Notice that when expressing **positive feelings** and **emotions** our **intonation** usually **varies** more than when we express negative feelings. For both **positive** and **negative feelings**, we **stress** the **key word/s** in the sentence.

c Underline the stressed words/syllables in these sentences. Tick (✓) the ones that you think will have more varied intonation.

1 ☐ I love it.
2 ☐ It's really rewarding.
3 ☐ I'm really fed up.
4 ☐ That's fantastic!
5 ☐ My job is very demanding.
6 ☐ I'd say my job is quite challenging.

d 🔊49 Listen to check your answers. Then listen and practise.

4 Work with a partner. If you work, tell your partner how you feel about your current job. If you don't work, tell your partner how you would feel about doing the jobs in exercise 1. Use words and phrases from the function focus.

75

exam expert

Interactive phase

Taking control over the interaction

5a Complete the advice about the interactive phase with words from the box.

> explore   in control   last   questions   start

In the interactive phase, the examiner may ¹.................... the conversation by saying something which invites an opinion, advice or recommendation. Remember that this phase needs to ².................... for four minutes – and that the candidate is ³.................... of the conversation! So it's a good idea to ⁴.................... the theme of the examiner's prompt by asking ⁵.................... before giving your viewpoint.

b 🎧 50 Listen to two candidates in the interactive phase responding to the same prompt from the examiner. How many questions does each candidate ask before giving their viewpoint?

Candidate 1 ....
Candidate 2 ....

c 🎧 50 Listen again and note down the questions that Candidate 1 asks.

d Work with a partner. Write at least five questions you could ask about the themes.

1 I have a few days here before I go back to England. Is there anything interesting to see?
2 I'm thinking of studying something new, but I'm not really sure what.
3 I need some advice about a present. I have to go to a birthday party next week but I don't know the person very well.

e Work with a partner. One of you is Student A, the other Student B. Follow the instructions.

Student A

Stage 1 You're the examiner, Student B is the candidate. Introduce a theme from d) and respond to the questions the candidate asks you.

Stage 2 You're the candidate, Student B is the examiner. Explore the theme that the examiner introduces by asking the questions you prepared for that theme in d).

Student B

Stage 1 You're the candidate, Student B is the examiner. Explore the theme that the examiner introduces by asking the questions you prepared for that theme in d).

Stage 2 You're the examiner, Student A is the candidate. Introduce a theme from d) and respond to the questions the candidate asks you.

f Decide with your partner how the conversations went. What did you do well? What could you improve? Ask your teacher, too.

The world of work

Reading

6a Work in pairs. Discuss these questions.

1 What do you think is a good age to start your working life? Give reasons.
2 Do teenagers in your country usually have a part-time job? Why/Why not?
3 Have you heard of any young people who have become very successful and made lots of money? How have they done it?

b Read the text. Answer question 3 above about the young businessman mentioned in it.

c Read the text again and note the five pieces of information that you find most interesting.

d Work in pairs. Tell your partner what you noted in c). Are they the same as your partner's?

e Could you be a young entrepreneur? Decide with your partner, using information from the text.

Writing

ISE Reading into Writing

➡ *See Writing file on pages 92–109.*

7 Read the text again and then, in your own words, write an article (approximately 250 words) for the students' website at your university:

i) summarising how Fraser Doherty became a successful young businessman **and**
ii) saying what you think are the positive and negative impacts of such early success on a young person's life.

TEENAGE SELF-MADE MILLIONAIRES – HOW DO THEY DO IT?

Fraser Doherty has been running his business since he was 14, when he started making jams from his grandmother's recipes in Edinburgh, Scotland. Originally, his customer base was just neighbours and friends, but business picked up quickly, and by age 16, he left school to work on his jams full time.

He perfected his recipes and came up with a name for his product: SuperJam. Orders started to come in faster than he could produce the jam in his parents' kitchen, so Doherty started renting time at a factory a few days each month.

His big break came in 2007, when one of the big UK supermarkets started stocking Superjam in its stores across the UK. Since then, other supermarket chains have followed and the company is now estimated to be worth between $1 and $2 million. Not bad for a 19-year-old.

Doherty's recommendation to other young entrepreneurs is: 'Have an attitude of adventure, and enjoy the journey'. But is that really enough to become super successful at such a young age? In a recent book on this subject, *50 Interviews: Young Entrepreneurs, What It Takes To Make More Than Your Parents*, seven factors were identified as being common to the young businesspeople who were interviewed:

1 They got emotional support and encouragement from their families.
2 They started with an idea that was manageable.
3 They work hard and don't give up.
4 They sacrifice their childhoods.
5 They were motivated by being told they wouldn't be successful.
6 They kept personal and business lives separate.
7 They were good at selling from an early age.

So is entrepreneurship something you're born with or just luck – being in the right place at the right time? Perhaps it's a mixture of the two, combined with another important factor: passion for what you do, not for money. As Fraser Doherty says, 'I can't be preoccupied with the money. I make jam because it's what I love to do.'

77

UNIT 11

Grammar focus

Present Perfect Continuous

To talk about actions or situations that started in the past and continue into the present we use:
has/have ('s/'ve) + (not) + been + verb + ing.

Fraser Doherty **has been running** his business **since** he was 14.
They**'ve been living** here **for** six months now.
What **have** you **been doing since** you left university last year?

Notice the use of **for** and **since** with the Present Perfect Continuous.
Remember:
for = to talk about the length or period of time
since = to talk about the point in time when something started

We use the Present Perfect Continuous instead of the Present Perfect Simple:
1 When we want to talk about more temporary situations and actions.
Compare:
I**'ve lived** here all my life.
I**'ve been living** here since last year.

2 When we want to emphasise the continuation or duration of an activity/situation, rather than its completion or outcome.
Compare:
I**'ve been working** here for eight months.
I**'ve had** three pay rises in eight months.

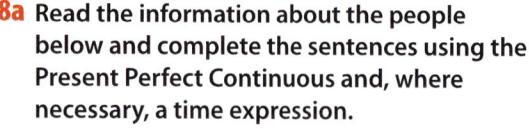

8a Read the information about the people below and complete the sentences using the Present Perfect Continuous and, where necessary, a time expression.

1. John works for Supersave Supermarket, as a trainee manager. He started there last summer.
   John...

2. Julie is waiting outside the cinema for her friend. She arrived an hour ago.
   Julie...

3. Bob and Sally live in Brighton. They moved there in 2010.
   Bob and Sally..

4. Elena is lying in bed. She went back to bed this morning because she felt ill.
   Elena...

5. Freddy is doing his homework. He started it three hours ago.
   Freddy..

6. Peter and Rosemary are having problems. The problems began about six months ago.
   Peter and Rosemary.....................................

b Prepare at least five questions to ask a partner about aspects of her/his life, using the Present Perfect Continuous.

How long have you been studying English?
What have you been doing recently?

c Ask your partner the questions you prepared in b).

exam expert

Topic phase

■ **Anticipating and answering questions**

9a Look back at the advice on page 59 to help you choose a topic, then make a mind map for your topic using information about how to do this from page 63. Bring your mind map and notes to your next class.

b Work with a partner. Swap mind maps and read the points your partner has made about her/his topic. Then plan at least six questions to ask her/him to find out more about the topic.

c One of you is Student A, the other Student B. Follow the instructions to roleplay the Topic phase in the exam.

Student A

Stage 1 You're the candidate. Lead a discussion about your topic, using the mind map and notes from 9a. The examiner (Student B) will ask you some questions about the topic. Be prepared to explain further and clarify any points you make.

Stage 2 You're the examiner. The candidate (Student B) is going to lead a discussion about her/his topic. Use the questions you prepared in 9b to ask for more information about the topic.

Student B

Stage 1 You're the examiner. The candidate (Student A) is going to lead a discussion about her/his topic. Use the questions you prepared in 9b to ask for more information about the topic.

Stage 2 You're the candidate. Lead a discussion about your topic, using the mind map and notes from 9a. The examiner (Student A) will ask you some questions about the topic. Be prepared to explain further and clarify any points you make.

Writing

ISE Portfolio/CW

➡ *See Writing file on pages 92–109.*

10 Choose one, or more, of these writing tasks.

Correspondence *(ISE II 2008)*
Today you overheard two colleagues planning to do something dishonest at work. Write an urgent email to the Chief Executive reporting what you heard and discussing what might happen if immediate action is not taken.

Factual writing
Write a report for your university website about job prospects for young people in your area. Give information about opportunities in different sectors and advice about what young people should do to maximise their chances of finding work.

Creative/descriptive writing *(ISE II 2009)*
Write a short story for a writing competition that begins or ends with the words, *I couldn't believe my luck. I never thought this would happen to me.*

Examiner: What would your dream job be?
Candidate: If I could do any job, I'd like to be a research scientist. I think it would be really interesting to work on trying to discover cures for illnesses, and really rewarding, too.

UNIT 12
Unexplained phenomena & events

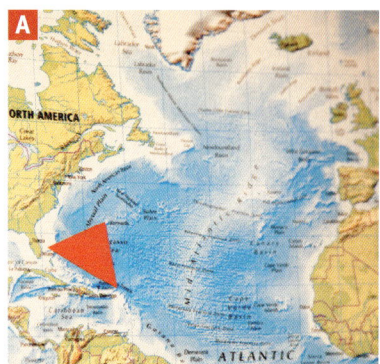

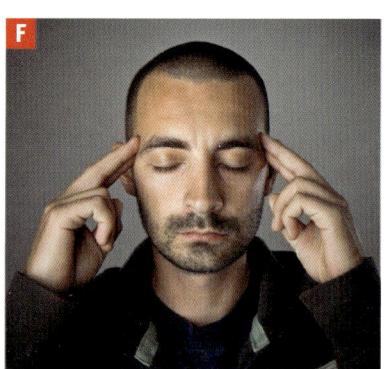

Vocabulary

1 Match the photos (A-F) to the different phenomena below (1-6).

1. ☐ telepathy
2. ☐ clairvoyance
3. ☐ haunted house
4. ☐ crop circles
5. ☐ the Bermuda triangle
6. ☐ alien abduction

Listening

2a 🎧 51 Match the conversations about strange experiences (1-6) to the photos (A-F).

b Have you heard any stories of strange events similar to the photos above? Tell a partner. Do you believe these stories?

c Read the recording script and listen to the recording again. Put the words and phrases below into the correct column of the table according to how they are used.

> maybe   supposedly   I've heard (that)...
> even though   perhaps   they/people say (that)...
> apparently   it could/may/might be
> although   in spite of   though

Expressing doubt and speculating

Joining contrasting ideas

Unexplained phenomena & events

Grammar focus

Speculating

1 We can use adverbs, such as *apparently* and *supposedly*, to show that we are not sure that what we are saying is completely true.
Apparently there are aliens landing on Earth all the time.

These adverbs can come in different positions in a sentence.
Apparently, she communicated through telepathy all her life.
She **apparently** communicated through telepathy all her life.
She communicated through telepathy all her life, **apparently**.

N.B. In perfect tenses adverbs are positioned like this:
She has **apparently** been able to communicate through telepathy all her life.

2 We can use expressions to show that what we are saying is not necessarily our opinion. This adds doubt.
People say the circles are made by alien space ships.
I've heard that she can see into the future and tell you what is going to happen.

3 We can use modal verbs to speculate about something that we are not sure about.
It's an old house. They **could** simply be noises as the house cools down in the evening.
He **may/might** have a special sort of power that means he can hear what you are saying.

If we are speculating about the past, we use a perfect tense after the modal verb:
I don't know, but she **might have disappeared** in a space ship.

4 There are other adverbs you can use to speculate about something and to show that what we are saying is a guess or an idea.
Maybe there are ghosts in the house. You haven't ever lived there.
Perhaps farmers are making the circles themselves.
She **possibly** uses things that she can see to tell your fortune, like the way you dress.

3a Rewrite the sentences using the word given to add doubt.

1. He can tell you what you are thinking. (*apparently*)
2. The plane disappeared while flying through the triangle. (*heard*)
3. The house has ghosts. (*people*)
4. When the photos were developed, you could see ghosts behind them. (*supposedly*)
5. There were UFOs sighted over the city last night. (*they*)
6. The police use clairvoyants sometimes to solve mystery cases. (*apparently*)

b Rewrite the sentences with the words supplied in the correct order.

1. she/train/missed/maybe/the
2. saw/happen/possibly/she/it/dream/a/in
3. may/made/corn/patterns/themselves/the/they/have
4. explanation/there/perhaps/is/a/simple
5. accident/boat/sunk/have/could/by/the
6. just/may/it/be/noisy/house/a

UNIT 12

c Work in pairs. Take it in turns to explain what has happened in these situations. Think of as many reasons as you can to explain what has happened, and use different expressions to speculate about the cause.

1. A friend of yours has arrived in class with a suntan.
2. Your teacher has not turned up for class.
3. Your wallet is not in your bag/pocket.
4. You have left a message on a friend's answering machine inviting them to a party, but they have not replied.
5. Suddenly all the lights in your classroom go out. It is completely dark.

b Read the magazine article again. Decide if the statements are true (T), false (F), or if the information is not given (NG).

1. ☐ The lines cover an area of 500 square metres.
2. ☐ Lines like this are found in other parts of the world.
3. ☐ We are sure the lines follow underground streams.
4. ☐ There are more than 50 different designs.
5. ☐ We are sure the lines were made by using the sun.
6. ☐ One of the figures is in the shape of an alien.

Reading

4a Read the article about the Nazca Lines once. Is the article definite about why and how they were made?

NAZCA LINES: ARE THEY A MYSTERY?

They are geometrically perfect and totally fascinating, but are these incredible formations the work of an enthusiastic ancient community working alone or is there a more mysterious explanation?

The Nazca Lines are a series of ancient geoglyphs (drawings on the ground made by moving stones) in the Peruvian desert over an area of 500 square kilometres. The designs include many straight lines as well as over 70 figures in the shape of animals and plants including: a spider, a hummingbird, a monkey, a lizard, a cactus and many more.

There are many theories about their purpose. Some people believe they are astronomical calendars or that they have a religious significance for example, that animal figures were sites where people worshipped water gods. Some scientists say the straight lines running for kilometres follow underground rivers. One of the more outlandish claims is that the lines are landing strips for alien aircraft. No one yet has come to a definitive answer.

There is also speculation about how they were made. The figures and lines are only visible from above and are made by turning over stones to reveal white soil beneath. This leads some people to believe that they may have been done from hot air balloons or even with the help of aliens. The most likely answer is that people used simple surveying tools and the rising and setting sun to map out the straight lines and shapes.

Whatever the answers, they are a wonderful sight, one of the most visited places in Peru and a UNESCO World Heritage site.

Unexplained phenomena & events

Writing

ISE Reading into Writing

➡ *See Writing file on pages 92-109.*

5 Refer to the article about the Nazca Lines. Write an article (approximately 250 words) for a school magazine:

i) summarising in your own words what the article says **and**

ii) speculating about why you think they were made.

Phonology

Using sentence stress to speculate

6a (52) Listen and circle the word or words that are stressed the most.

1 She can apparently tell people's fortunes.
2 They say that hundreds of cars have disappeared.
3 The marks are supposedly done by aliens.
4 I've heard that there are none left.
5 People say that the house has a ghost.

b Use words and expressions to add doubt to these sentences. Practise pronouncing them with a partner.

1 He can read people's palms.
2 He was taken by aliens.
3 They can talk to each other without speaking.
4 There are ghosts in that building.
5 A plane disappeared last night in the Bermuda triangle.

exam expert

Topic phase

More concerns about your topic

7a (53) Listen to a candidate expressing her concerns about her topic presentation. Tick the concerns she mentions in the list below.

1 She has too much to talk about.
2 She will forget what to say.
3 She will pronounce some words incorrectly.
4 Her topic sounds boring.
5 She doesn't know everything about the topic.
6 She has too many photos to take into the exam.

b Follow these instructions.

- Write a list of the things that you think might cause problems in your exam.
- Share your thoughts with a partner.
- Now practise talking about your topic with your partner.
- Listen for things that your partner is worried about while they talk and then give some feedback.
- Think about your partner's feedback. What can you do about your concerns?

exam expert

Conversation phase

Keeping the conversation going

8a In the Conversation phase for Grade 8, the examiner will choose two subjects from the following list. (For ISE II there will be these six subjects and another six.) Match a question (1-6) with each subject (A-F).

A National environmental concerns
B Unexplained phenomena and events
C Public figures
D Society and living standards
E The world of work
F Personal values and ideals

1 ☐ What kinds of jobs do you think won't be required in 20 years time?
2 ☐ Do you think that famous people have a right to privacy?
3 ☐ In films there are many characters with magical powers. Do you think it is possible for people to have these powers in real life?
4 ☐ What do you think are the most important environmental issues in your country?
5 ☐ What kind of things do you value in a friend?
6 ☐ Have people's lifestyles changed recently in your country? Are people better off?

b 🎧 54 One way of keeping a conversation going is by providing longer answers. Listen to the answers to the questions from a). What extra information does the candidate give? Choose A, B or C.

1 Personal values and ideals
   A She has always valued her education.
   B She has always valued her friends.
   C She will definitely value her health.
2 Public figures
   A Too much money is wasted on famous people.
   B Famous people are just like us.
   C Famous people have no privacy at home.

3 Unexplained phenomena or events
   A He likes superhero films.
   B It would be good to have super powers.
   C Intuition could be another sense.
4 National environmental concerns
   A Her city restricts traffic in the centre.
   B There are no cars in the city centre.
   C There is more public transport.
5 The world of work
   A We can't live without computers.
   B The Internet is very important.
   C We will work less in the future.
6 Society and living standards
   A Shops open for more hours.
   B People spend less money.
   C People don't go shopping anymore.

c In pairs, write down three questions you could ask for each of the topics listed in a).

d Change partners. One of you is the candidate and the other is the examiner. Your teacher will call out a subject.

Student A: you are the examiner, ask the questions you have written for that subject.

Student B: you are the candidate, answer the questions, giving extra information each time.

Keep going until your teacher changes the subject.

84

exam expert

Interactive phase

Encouraging comments

Sometimes asking someone to comment on what you have been talking about can be a way of keeping the conversation going when it has come to an end. You will explore the conversation more and it can give you more opportunities to ask new questions.

9a 🎧55 Listen to these parts of conversations. Write down the exact questions the people use to invite comments.

1 ....
....
....

2 ....
....
....

b Match the beginnings and endings of the questions and find other ways of inviting comment.

1 ☐ What do you
2 ☐ Have you ever experienced
3 ☐ What would you have
4 ☐ What's your
5 ☐ Have you ever been

A something like that?
B opinion about it?
C think about it?
D in a situation like that?
E done in a situation like that?

c Work in pairs and follow these instructions.

- Write notes about a strange event you have heard about.
- Practice telling the short story together.
- Find a new partner and tell your story.
- Partners, comment on the story you have heard.
- After your partner has commented, ask more questions about what they have said to keep the conversation going.

Writing

ISE Portfolio/CW

➡ See Writing file on pages 92-109.

10 Choose one, or more, of these writing tasks.

Correspondence (ISE II 2009)

You have received an email from your Scottish friend who lives in an old house. She is frightened because she thinks her house might be haunted and that there is a ghost in the attic. Write an email to your friend expressing your concerns and advising her how to deal with the situation.

Factual writing (ISE II 2008)

You recently met a fortune teller, Eva Kay, who looks into her crystal ball and predicts the future for people. Write an article for a family magazine, describing what she told you about your future and what your reaction was. Say how far you think such forecasts can be trusted.

Creative/descriptive writing (ISE II 2011)

Write a story for a writing competition beginning with the words, *If I hadn't overslept and been late, I would never have had such an exciting encounter.*

Examiner: Why do you think that people enjoy mysteries?
Candidate: Well, I'm not really sure. **Apparently**, near where I live, some farmers' animals have disappeared overnight. **They say that** something takes them. I don't really believe it is anything mysterious. **Maybe** they're stolen by someone.

Review Units 10-12

1 Re-order the words to make sentences and questions.

1. not/me/about/worry/to/it/told/she
2. a/working/I/have/been/here/year/for
3. long/have/been/you/living/here/how?
4. they/ask/didn't/if/I/seen/had/before/it
5. heard/there/that/that/are/in/house/ghosts/have/you?
6. she/hear/apparently/thoughts/your/can
7. are/they/perhaps/aliens/made/by
8. hadn't/Frank/driving/long/been/car/stopped/when/the
9. made/explained/he/how/cheese/was

2 Complete the sentences with one of the verbs supplied (some can be used more than once).

> told   promised   doubt   heard   asked
> discussed   say   think   said

1. I .... he'll come. He's been working so hard lately he never goes out.
2. She .... me to be careful. They've been cleaning the floor and it is slippery.
3. I don't .... I'd like a job that didn't have any responsibility. I like to be in charge.
4. She .... that we should study all six units to prepare for the exam.
5. They .... that it is expensive to live there. I don't know if it is true or not.
6. I .... that he disappeared and never came back. Do you think it's true?
7. We .... if other people had seen ghosts as well.
8. He .... to take him on holiday to the Caribbean.

3 Choose the correct answer (A or B) to complete the gap.

1. I really don't know what got into her. .... crazy and slapped her friend in the face.
   A She went apparently
   B She apparently went

2. It's one of the oldest things in this museum. A priest .... it in the 12th century.
   A made supposedly
   B supposedly made

3. They .... the island and went to another place when the food ran out. We don't really know it was so long ago.
   A might leave
   B might have left

4. A: 'What do you think is eating the lettuce in the garden. Each morning there is less and less.'
   B: 'It .... a rabbit. We'll have to stay up and watch to find out.'
   A could be
   B can be

5. The old man has .... able to tell the future since she was a little boy.
   A been apparently
   B apparently been

6. .... that they were made by local tribes long ago but I don't believe them.
   A I say
   B People say

Review units 10-12

What do you remember about the Written Portfolio and the Controlled Written examination?

4 Decide if the following sentences are true or false. Can you correct the false ones?

The Portfolio

1 Each year there is a list of topics for the portfolio published on the Trinity website.
2 You can either choose the topics listed for your year or any others from previous years.
3 The types of tasks include: correspondence (letters and emails), factual writing (reports, articles and reviews), creative and descriptive writing (stories, diary entries, descriptions).
4 The word limits are all the same for each type – 170 to 200 words.
5 Your portfolio must contain three pieces of writing. One from each type.

The Controlled written examination

1 There are two tasks in the controlled written examination.
2 There is no choice given. You must complete the written tasks given to you.
3 The tasks have an uneven weighting, 60% and 40%.
4 You have 90 minutes to complete the writing tasks.
5 Task 1 is a reading into writing task where you are asked to comment specifically about an article provided and then give your own views and opinions about something related to the article.
6 Task 2 will be a writing task that asks for a certain style of writing appropriate to the types in the portfolio e.g. correspondence, factual or creative and descriptive writing.
7 Both tasks should be about 200 words long.

Exam tips – Written exam

1 Practise writing tests of the exam length to get a feeling for how long this is. Work out how many words you write per page so you don't waste time in the exam counting words!

2 There are two tasks and you must complete each one – you don't get a choice of what to write. Try to give the same amount of time to each task.

Units 10-12 Self-evaluation

Write Y (yes) or N (needs more practice) for each statement.

1 ☐ I can talk about society and living standards.
2 ☐ I can talk about the world of work.
3 ☐ I can talk about unexplained phenomena and events.
4 ☐ I can report what others have said.
5 ☐ I can emphasise an event's duration or the fact that it is not finished yet using the Present Perfect Continuous.
6 ☐ I can speculate and express doubt.

Now you write 'can do' statements like the ones above for the interactive and communicative skills you have practised in Units 10-12.

The following section provides examples of the types of examiner and candidate language for different parts of the exam.

1 Focus on the Topic phase

In this phase you will talk about a topic that you have prepared for. Here is an example for the Grade 8 exam.

Getting ready

Examiner: We're going to start the topic phase now. What have you chosen for your topic?
Candidate: I've prepared to talk about one of my favourite places, the British Museum in London. I have been there a couple of times and I love it.

Examiner: Do you have any notes or materials that you are going to use?
Candidate: Yes, I have some notes and also some material I have collected when visiting. Here is a copy of my notes.

Starting

Examiner: Great. So let's get started. Why have you chosen this topic in particular? What is it about the museum that attracts you most.
Candidate: Well, I thought I should choose something that interests me and I am studying art history at university, so the British Museum is a great place for people like me. I'm sure you can go there more than twenty times and still see new things. Also, it has some of the most amazing things from all over the world and therefore there is something for everyone no matter if you are interested in jewellery, sculpture, paintings, craft. Whatever you like, you'll find something.

Spontaneous discussion

Candidate: ... and one of the most famous and perhaps controversial pieces are the Greek marbles and the Egyptian mummies. And it's the Egyptian mummies that I'm most interested in.
Examiner: I haven't heard of the Greek marbles. Why do you say they are controversial?
Candidate: Well, they are statues taken from the Parthenon in Athens a long time ago – I'm not sure exactly when – and taken to the UK. Greece would like the marbles returned and have even built a museum to house them. But the UK currently refuses to return them. They say that the marbles wouldn't exist if it wasn't for the British Museum. Have you ever seen them?
Examiner: Yes, once. Maybe. I think I know the ones you mean. What is your opinion about them? Do you think they should be returned?
Candidate: Well I'm not completely sure. I believe it is likely that the marbles wouldn't exist at all if the British hadn't taken them but I can also see that Greece believes they were stolen and should be returned. But that would call into question a lot of the content in many museums around the world. If I was Greek though, I'm sure I'd want them back.

Trinity Takeaway

2 Focus on the Interactive phase

In this phase, you will talk about a topic that the examiner introduces. However, the candidate is responsible for taking control of the conversation and keeping the discussion going.

Getting ready

Examiner: We're going to start the Interactive phase now. I'm going to introduce a topic and we'll speak about it together.
Candidate: OK.

Prompt 1 (Grade 7)

Examiner: One of my old school friends is organising a party to meet up with all the people who were in our class at school. But I'm not sure I want to go.
Candidate: Oh really. I went to a party like that once. I had a good time. Why do you think you won't like it?
Examiner: Well there are a lot of people it would be good to see but there are some people that I've lost contact with and I would feel strange seeing them again.
Candidate: Yes, I know how you might feel. Could be strange being there with some people that you used to spend a lot of time with but that you haven't seen for a long time. But on the other hand, it could be an opportunity too... I don't know how to say this in English... to become friends again with them.
Examiner: Yes, that's true. Do you have any friends from school that you don't see anymore?
Candidate: Oh yes, lots. I finished school only a year ago and there are already people that I don't contact anymore. But maybe that is part of life. You know, your interests change and you have different priorities. Do you think there will be a lot of people at the party?
Examiner: I'm not sure. But my friend says that she has invited everyone who used to be in our class. That would be about 60 people.
Candidate: 60 people is a lot. If they all came, it would be difficult to speak to everyone. So maybe it won't be so bad. If there are some people that come that you don't want to talk to much, you could talk to others.

Prompt 2 (Grade 8)

Examiner: I'm a bit tired of my job and am thinking of making a career change. But I have no idea where to start.
Candidate: Really. Don't you like being an examiner?
Examiner: Oh, yes. Of course I do. But I only do this part time. My other job is as a writer.
Candidate: Wow. That's great. I had a friend who was a writer. He said it was a great job. What don't you like about it? I imagine it would be an interesting and creative job.
Examiner: Well I've been doing it for a while now and it can take up a lot of time. It's not really a nine to five job. You've always got something to think about.
Candidate: Yes. I've never thought about it like that. I suppose it could become tiring after a while. Always having something you should be doing. Like you're never able to relax. Like being a student and always having homework or reading to do.

Trinity Takeaway

3 Focus on the Conversation phase

In the conversation phase for **GESE Grades 7 & 8** you will talk about two of the subject areas from the six on the syllabus. Again, while the areas are chosen by the examiner, the candidate needs to demonstrate that they can take an active role in keeping the conversation going.

Grade 7

Examiner: Now we're into the last phase. The Conversation phase, where we talk about two of the topic areas. So let's start off with education. What type of school did you go to?

Candidate: I went to a local primary and secondary school in my town. It wasn't a big town so the school was small and it was co-educational. I liked it because you knew everyone there.

Examiner: What about your teachers, did you have a favourite?

Candidate: I liked all of my teachers really but I remember that my grade 5 teacher was lots of fun. She used to play the guitar and teach us songs in class. We loved that... So what about you? What was it like where you grew up?

Examiner: Well... there wasn't much to do around where I lived. But that didn't stop us from having fun. On the weekend we used to disappear in the mornings on our bikes and wouldn't come back until after dark.

Grade 8

Examiner: OK. Let's talk about another topic now. How about the natural environment? Are you concerned about the natural environment in your country?

Candidate: I am, but it's not my main concern. I know a lot of people that spend time recycling, joining groups that clean up the local area and stuff but I don't do that much. I do what I can at home, but I don't think I go to any special effort. I'm more concerned about other topics.

Examiner: Oh. What things are you more concerned about?

Candidate: Well, I trust that our local government are doing a lot about recycling and things like that. So I prefer to spend my time on other things. For example, I'm interested in people's rights...

Examiner: Why do you think that people enjoy mysteries?

Candidate: Well, I'm not sure really. Apparently near where I live, some farmers' animals have disappeared overnight. They say that something takes them. I don't really believe it is anything mysterious. Maybe they're stolen by someone.

Trinity Takeaway

The interview for **ISE II** is the same as the interview for GESE Grades 7 & 8 but in the third section – the Conversation phase – you will speak about your portfolio and one subject area.

Discussion of portfolio

Getting started

Examiner: First of all we're going to talk about your portfolio tasks. I see the first one is a review. What made you interested in writing a review?

Candidate: Well, when we were choosing our tasks, I had just been to see a play at my local theatre and other people in the class were reviewing films they had seen. So I thought this would be a bit different.

Taking the conversation further

Examiner: So tell me about this play. Your review is quite positive but you mention that other reviewers didn't like it.

Candidate: Yes, I enjoyed it. But I was surprised that it didn't get such great reviews in local newspapers. I thought that the acting and the stage were really good so I tried to show that in my review. The stage designer used very little on the stage. It was all white apart from a few coloured steps and blocks. I thought this was really effective but I think it was this that the reviewers didn't like.

Repairing a breakdown in communication

Examiner: I'm confused. So are you saying that they thought the staging didn't help?

Candidate: Sort of, but not exactly. I think that the other reviewers preferred a set that supported the actors more. You know, a more traditional house if they are in a house, garden if they are in a garden. I think they thought that this would help the actors be more realistic. I didn't mind the acting. But I think the reviewers thought the actors would do better in a more realistic stage.

Writing file

Correspondence – informal letters

ISE II Controlled Written (approx. 250 words), Portfolio Section 1 (120-150 words)

Purpose (examples)	- to give/ask for advice/make suggestions - to explain/describe a situation/event/experience - to give reasons for something - to express how you feel about something
Typical readers	- a friend - a member of your family
Organisation of text	- organisation flexible, but you should think about the information you need to include and organise it logically
Features	- sender's address optional; don't include recipient's address - appropriate salutation, e.g. *Dear*, *Hi*, and ending, e.g. *From*, *Love*, - date optional. If included, it should be above the opening salutation - language style: informal to neutral - language structures and functions: depend on purpose of letter, e.g. past tenses to describe an experience you had

1a Read the Portfolio task and sample answer. What positive influence did Jim's teacher have on him?

A teacher who had a very positive influence on you has just retired. Write a letter to this teacher explaining in what ways they influenced your personal values and speculating how your life would have been different if they had not been your teacher. (ISE II Portfolio Task 2010)

3 West Street
Lewes
East Sussex

20 February 2011

Dear Mrs Wallace,

How are you? I've just heard that you've retired. What wonderful news this is for you. I thought I'd take this chance to let you know that you were one of the teachers I remember most. When I was in your grade 6 class I was going through a hard time at home and with some of the children at school. This was making my life quite unbearable. I'll never forget the kind attention and help you gave me. You were so understanding when I couldn't complete my work and you helped me a lot with advice on how to handle my classmates. This made a real difference and helped me to understand how to be generous and kind to all people. If you hadn't been my teacher, I am sure that I wouldn't have been able to start secondary school that year.

All the very best on your new adventure,

Kind regards

Jim

Writing file

b Analyse the letter by completing the table below. Refer to the information about informal letters to help you.

Purpose	
Readers	
Organisation of text	Salutation – *Dear/Kind regards* Paragraph 1 – … Paragraph 2 – *the reason why they are writing* Paragraph 3 – …
Features	language features: e.g. contractions (*couldn't*) tone and style

c In pairs, think of some ways that teachers can help and inspire their students. What kinds of positive things can you remember from past teachers?

d Now write your own version of the letter. Use some of the ideas you thought of in c). Follow these steps for drafting and editing your work.

Steps

1. Write a first draft; check the word limit.
2. Use the Self Assessment Checklist and make any necessary corrections.
3. Use the same Checklist to help a partner check her/his work.
4. Write a second draft. Use your partner's suggestions to improve your work.
5. Give your text to the teacher. Use her/his Checklist to improve your work.
6. Make a final draft of the text, taking into account your teacher's suggestions.

2 In pairs, use the table in exercise 1a) to plan one of the tasks below. Remember to use the steps from d) above.

1

Your friend is planning to open a shop for tourists in your area. Write a letter to your friend suggesting some local products that he could sell and saying why you think they would be popular with tourists. Say how successful you think the shop will be. (ISE II 2011)

2

You receive a letter from an old friend who you have not seen for many years suggesting you go on an adventure holiday together. However, you are not sure about it for a variety of reasons. Write a diplomatic email to your friend explaining how you feel and suggest meeting to discuss it. (ISE II 2007)

Writing file

Correspondence – emails

ISE II Controlled Written (approx. 250 words) Portfolio Section 1 (120-150 words)

> You can choose to write an email or a letter for any of the tasks in this section. However, if the task requires a more formal tone, it would be more appropriate to write it in the format of a formal letter, rather than an email.

Purpose (examples)	• to give/ask for advice/make suggestions • to explain/describe a situation/event/experience • to give reasons for something • to express how you feel about something
Typical readers	• a friend • a member of your family
Organisation of text	• there isn't a 'correct' way, but make sure you organise the information you need to include logically
Features	• must be produced on email software and printed out • complete the 'subject line' (the space appears automatically) • date can be in your own language (it's generated automatically) • don't use text-message spelling, but you can use common abbreviations, e.g. asap (as soon as possible), and emoticons, e.g. ☺ • salutations at beginning are optional depending on how well you know the person • sign off in some way, e.g. with your name

1a Read this email version of the informal letter on page 92. Are there any differences in the message?

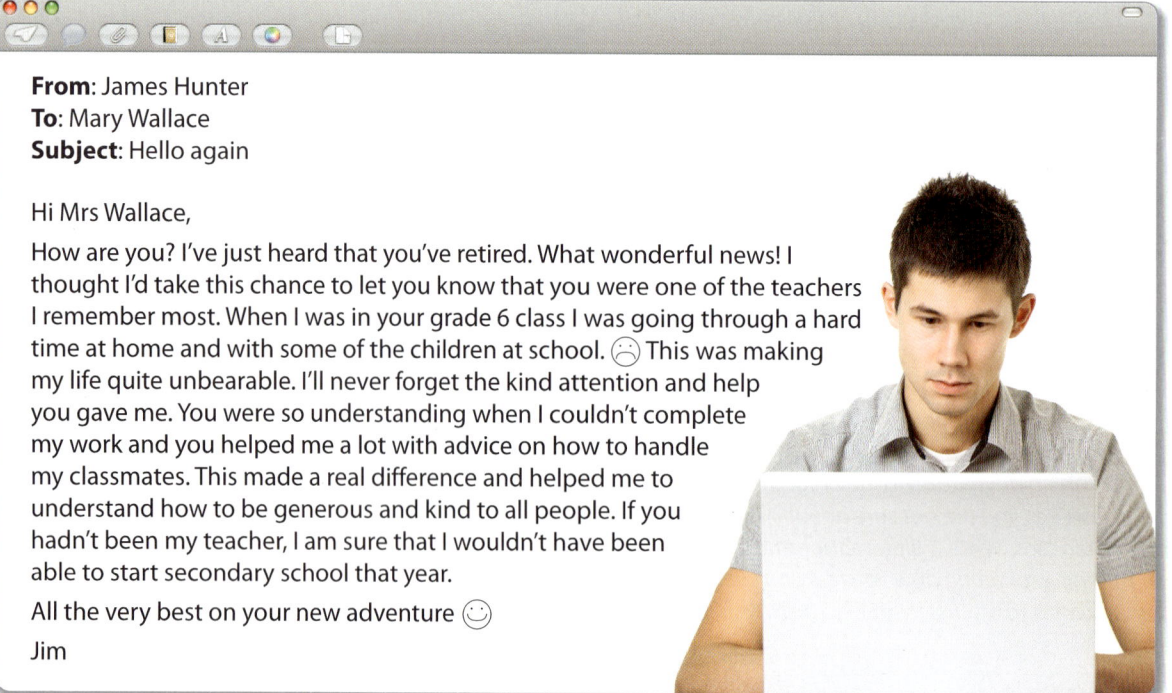

From: James Hunter
To: Mary Wallace
Subject: Hello again

Hi Mrs Wallace,

How are you? I've just heard that you've retired. What wonderful news! I thought I'd take this chance to let you know that you were one of the teachers I remember most. When I was in your grade 6 class I was going through a hard time at home and with some of the children at school. ☹ This was making my life quite unbearable. I'll never forget the kind attention and help you gave me. You were so understanding when I couldn't complete my work and you helped me a lot with advice on how to handle my classmates. This made a real difference and helped me to understand how to be generous and kind to all people. If you hadn't been my teacher, I am sure that I wouldn't have been able to start secondary school that year.

All the very best on your new adventure ☺

Jim

Writing file

b Find the differences between the format of the email and the letter. Compare your answers with a partner.

letter	email
sender's address	no postal address

c Now change your own version of this task (from Informal letters, exercise 1d) into an email, making any necessary changes.

d Swap emails with a partner and check your partner's message. Has your partner made the necessary changes?

2 In pairs, use the table from exercise 1b) to plan one of the tasks below. Remember to use the steps from Informal letters 1d).

1

You have recently accepted the job of your dreams, but it is a long way from your family and friends. Write an email to a friend you have left behind explaining how your life has changed and how you have been feeling. (ISE II Portfolio Task 2009)

2

You have recently heard a speech given by a public figure in your country who you really admire. Write an email to your English friend telling her what the speaker talked about and describing your feelings about the whole experience. (ISE II Portfolio Task 2008)

Writing file

Correspondence – formal/neutral letters and emails

ISE II Controlled Written exam (approx. 250 words), Portfolio Section 1 (120-150 words)

Purpose (examples)	• to complain • to request action
Typical readers	• the person in charge of a business/other organisation • the person responsible for customer service • the editor of a newspaper or publication
Organisation of text	Formal letters have a standard layout and organisation: • sender's address goes at top (it can be indented to the right) • recipient's address goes at top (under the sender's address) • date goes below sender's address • subject heading goes after the opening salutation, on left or in centre of page • separate paragraph necessary for each theme Formal emails do not require the same amount of organisation as a letter: • sender's postal address is often found in an email signature at the end • recipient's postal address is not included • the date is registered automatically when sending • subject headings can appear like in a letter • separate paragraphs as necessary for each theme.
Features	• use standard salutation and ending, i.e. if *Dear Sir*, end with *Yours faithfully*; • if *Dear Mr Smith*, end with *Yours sincerely* • language style: neutral to formal for both letters and emails • language structures: depends on purpose of letter, e.g. in a letter to request action, this could involve making suggestions • language functions: depends on purpose of letter, e.g. in a letter of complaint, • this could involve expressing feelings and expressing disagreement

Writing file

1a Read the Portfolio task and sample answer below. What did Mr Hunter complain about?

Your local council has decided to cancel this year's festival in your area for reasons of public safety. It has taken place for over 100 years and you think it is an important event for the community. Write a letter to the council explaining why you think the festival should be allowed and suggesting measures to protect the public. (ISE II Portfolio Task 2009)

3 West Street
Lewes
East Sussex BN7 5DY

The Manager
Council Public Events Team
Lewes BN7 7SL

15 April 2010

Subject: Cancellation of Bonfire Night

Dear Sir,

I am writing to complain about your decision to cancel this year's bonfire night festival because of public safety.

This festival is a national event to remember the events of many hundreds of years ago, when there was a failed attempt to explode a bomb at parliament house in London. A bonfire, and more recently fireworks, have been supplied by the local council for over 100 years. Not providing this service centrally would break a very old tradition, deny residents the chance to celebrate as a community and increase the safety risk even more as residents themselves make fires in their own back gardens. Burns and accidents are more common at home on such a night than at controlled public events.

I would like to suggest that you listen to the views of local residents and consider solutions that could help maintain a safe public environment that we can all share.

I look forward to hearing from you.

Yours faithfully,

J Hunter
James Hunter

writing file

b What three reasons did Mr Hunter give for why the festival should not be cancelled?

c Analyse the letter by completing the table below.

Purpose	
Reader	
Organisation of text	Separate paragraph each theme: Paragraph 1 – *what the letter is about* Paragraph 2 – Paragraph 3 –
Features	Language and style...

d Now write your own version of the text in response to the task. Use an example of a local festival from where you live. Follow the steps below to help you draft and edit your letter.

Steps
1. Write a first draft; check the word limit.
2. Use the Self Assessment Checklist and make any necessary corrections.
3. Use the same Checklist to help a partner check her/his work.
4. Write a second draft. Use your partner's suggestions to improve your work.
5. Give your text to the teacher. Use her/his Checklist to improve your work.
6. Make a final draft of the text, taking into account your teacher's suggestions.

2 In pairs, use the table in exercise 1c) to plan one of the tasks below. Remember to use the steps from d).

1

When you were shopping at the supermarket recently, the assistant at the checkout was very rude to you. Write a letter to the supermarket manager, reporting what the assistant said, explaining how you felt and saying what action you think the manager should take. (ISE II Portfolio Task 2010)

2

You are concerned about the large amount of waste paper and rubbish that is produced in your school/workplace. Write a letter to your teacher/manager making specific suggestions on how things should be improved and try to persuade him of the seriousness of the situation. (ISE II Portfolio Task 2007)

Writing file

Factual Writing – reports

ISE II Controlled Written (approx. 250 words), Portfolio Section 2 (170-200 words)

If you are asked to write a report in the first part of the Controlled Written exam, you will need to include a summary of a text as part of your report. See the Skills for Reading into Writing (page 109) for help with summarising texts.

Purpose (examples)	• to give factual information about something, e.g. a subject, event, place, service
Typical readers	• readers of a specialist magazine, e.g. school/college magazine, food magazine
Organisation of text	• the report should have a title that describes the contents • start with a statement about what the report is about • you can use bullet points/headings to make organisation clear
Features	• language style: neutral to formal • usually more objective and factual than articles • text marking words like *below* and *above* can be used to talk about something you are going to say or have said • sequencing words are often used, e.g. *firstly*, *secondly*, *in conclusion* • often contains recommendations based on the facts presented

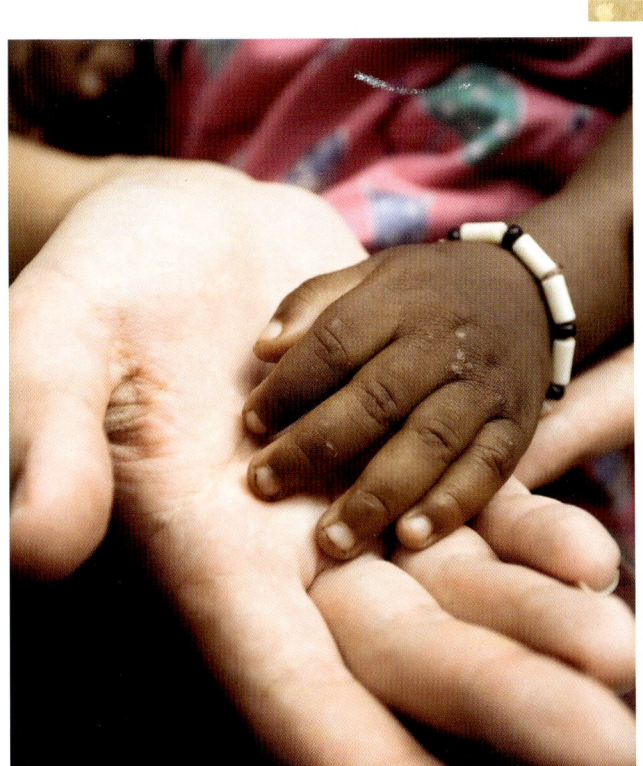

writing file

1a Read the Portfolio task and sample answer below, and write the correct headings (1-7) above the paragraphs in the report (A-E). There are two extra headings you do not need.

1 Enrich your experience
2 Forgetting about university
3 Losing money
4 Improve your CV
5 Seeing the world
6 Clear your head and think
7 Losing momentum

Write a report for an international student organisation about the value of gap years. Highlight the advantages and disadvantages of taking a year out from full-time education, and make some suggestions about possible activities students could do. (ISE II Portfolio Task 2010)

GAP YEARS: SHOULD YOU TAKE ONE?

Many students in the UK take a year's break (a gap year) after secondary school and delay their entry to university.

The advantages

A ....
- Firstly, many use the year as a chance to think, without the pressure of choosing a career or course of study.
- Gap-year takers can use their time to research what they really want to do and explore their skills and interests further.

B ....
- Additionally, gap years are used to learn something new.
- There are many opportunities for volunteer work in the UK and overseas and this opens doors to new experiences not available through study.

C ....
- Future employers are also interested in gap years.
- Demonstrating you have used your time well, learnt new skills and contributed to society are all positive signs for potential employers.
- There are special organisations that can arrange international volunteering for you.

The disadvantages

D ....
- Many parents are concerned that a gap year will distract their children and they will not return to university. It is true that some students do not return, however, most people do.

E ....
- Furthermore, some students taking a gap year are afraid of not being able to return to the student life. It can be difficult to get back into study and being poor if you have been working.
- There are special charities and counsellors at universities that can help students settle back in.

Overall, gap years can provide a welcome break and the chance for new experiences that many secondary school leavers cannot resist.

Writing file

b Decide with a partner if you think you would like to go on a gap year or not. What would you use the time to do?

c Read the report again then analyse it by completing the table below. Refer to the information about reports in the table above for help.

Purpose	
Readers	
Organisation of text	
Features	language style and tone

d Now write your own answer to the Portfolio task. Follow these steps for drafting and editing your report.

Steps

1. Write a first draft; check the word limit.
2. Use the Self Assessment Checklist and make any necessary corrections.
3. Use the same Checklist to help a partner check her/his work.
4. Write a second draft. Use your partner's suggestions to improve your work.
5. Give your text to the teacher. Use her/his Checklist to improve your work.
6. Make a final draft of the text, taking into account your teacher's suggestions.

2 In pairs, use the table in exercise 1c) to plan one of the tasks below. Remember to use the steps above to help you complete your text.

1

A beautiful building of historic importance is going to be demolished so that a new motorway can be built. Write a report for the department of transport persuading them to reconsider the decision. Explain why you disagree with the plan and recommend an alternative route for the motorway. (ISE II 2010)

2

You have been investigating social issues in your area. Write a report for the local council about the social problems in your area, giving examples of matters which have caused friction among neighbours. Make some suggestions for helping people to live together happily. (ISE II 2008)

writing file

Factual Writing – review

ISE II Controlled Written exam (approx. 250 words), Portfolio Section 2 (170-200 words)

Purpose (examples)	• to give factual information about a work of art (a painting, piece of music, book), performance (a play, film, dance), event (an exhibition, concert, fair) or place (a website, restaurant) • to give a personal opinion about how well the work was achieved
Typical readers	• a potential audience member • a reader of a magazine or a newspaper
Organisation of text	• start with factual information about the work, e.g. title or name, characters and actors, authors and artists. • for a work of art, describe what it is like; for a performance, what was played; for an event, what it included; for a place; what it was like • mention what was both good and bad about it • include your opinion and whether you recommend it or not • details about the dates, times, locations and how to get more information are often contained at the end of the review
Features	• language and style will depend on the type of magazine or newspaper and the audience. A more formal performance like an opera, for example, will have a more formal tone. • reviews will often include strong opinions using very expressive words, e.g. *superb*, *excellent*, *extremely poor*

1a Read the Portfolio task and sample answer on page 103, and answer the following questions.

1 Is the overall review positive or negative?
2 After reading this review, would you be encouraged to read it?

Write a review of your favourite children's book for a magazine feature on, 'The world's most popular books for children'. Include details of the story and main characters. Explain why you would recommend it to young readers.
(ISEII Portfolio task 2010)

102

Writing file

THE VERY HUNGRY CATERPILLAR KEEPS EATING

One of my favourite books as a child, and one I now love to read to my young children, is *The Very Hungry Caterpillar*, written and illustrated by Eric Carle. First published in 1969 the book is still in print today, more than 40 years later, and available in over 50 languages. I remember fondly how my mother and father used to read this story to me and how I eventually learned to read it for myself.

The story focuses on the journey of the main character, a caterpillar. As you might guess she is very hungry and spends the story eating her way through many different types of food, which grow in number on each page. What I like most, and the reason I would recommend it for young readers especially, is that it is a perfect way to teach numbers and the names of colours and food. Each page also includes a small hole through which the caterpillar goes, encouraging your children to guess what is on the next page.

The illustrations are particularly vivid, colourful and expressive, and some of the images are now iconic. The story ends with a bang and a breathtaking image that your child will love.

The Very Hungry Caterpillar is a must in every child's bookshelf and will provide years of enjoyment.

b Read the answer again and find these features of a review:

1. personal opinion
2. facts about the work itself (e.g. when it was written, who wrote it)
3. facts about the book (where it is available, what it is useful for)
4. examples of strong language to describe the work

What words, expressions and tenses are used to do these things?

c Now write your answer to the Portfolio task above.

2 With a partner, plan how you would answer the example portfolio tasks below. Use the features of a review in exercise 1b) to think about how you would answer the task.

1

Write a review for an educational magazine of a factual television programme which you think is outstanding. Explain what the programme is about, what people could learn from it and why you recommend it so highly. (ISE II Portfolio Task 2009)

2

The Arts Editor of a national newspaper has asked you to review two new books for teenagers, saying what you think is important in stories for this age group and how far you feel each of the books is successful in providing these qualities. (ISE II Portfolio Task 2008)

writing file

Factual Writing – article

ISE II Controlled Written exam (approx. 250 words), Portfolio Section 2 (170-200 words)

If you are asked to write an article in the first part of the Controlled Written exam, you will need to include a summary of a text as part of your article. See the section on writing summaries (page 109) to help you with summarising texts.

Purpose (examples)	• give information about something, e.g. a subject, event, place, service
Typical readers	• readers of a school/college magazine, travel magazine, newspaper • typically non-specialised readers
Organisation of text	• the article should have a title • articles reporting events often give factual information first • more general articles often start with an interesting statement that attracts the reader • the text is organised over a number of paragraphs
Features	Depends on the purpose of the article and reader: • language style: e.g. informal to neutral for popular magazines • language structures: e.g. past tenses to report events • language functions: e.g. language of advice if the article is giving • recommendations, language of instructions and directions if the article is describing how to do something

1a Read the Portfolio task below and the article written in response. Overall, does the writer believe that the woman will be successful?

For the first time in your region, a woman has recently become an important public figure. Write an article for an international news magazine, outlining her background and expressing the reaction of the general public to her appointment. Speculate about her future career. (ISE II Portfolio Task 2009)

> **First woman to hold post of Regional Minister for Education**
>
> 1 For the first time in our country's history, a woman has been selected as Education Minister. Dr Emilia Suarez now has the hopes and dreams of millions of primary and secondary school children in her hands.
>
> 2 Born in the small town of Merida, she was a star student and won a competitive scholarship to study languages at the National University. She excelled at university and won a further scholarship to complete post-graduate studies in the UK. Dr Suarez entered politics recently but has been a major force behind educational reform.
>
> 3 In her first press conference after the announcement Dr Suarez expressed her gratitude for the appointment but left no doubt about the challenge ahead. She said that we clearly face difficult economic times. However, now was the time to invest in our children's future. She went on to list her priorities which included introducing a minimum of four hours of physical education a week in all primary schools.
>
> 4 Public opinion is strong for Dr Suarez, especially among women voters. However, it remains to be seen whether Ms Suarez can be effective in what has been a male-dominated world. It is possible that her fresh approach will be popular, especially among the teacher community, where women dominate in the region and have been working hard to get representation at the top.

Writing file

b Match these descriptions of the purpose of each paragraph to the correct number.

A ☐ author's view of public opinion and how successful she might be
B ☐ the woman's background
C ☐ the event that article is about
D ☐ interesting facts about the immediate future

c Analyse the article on page 104 by completing the table below. Refer to the information about articles above for help.

Purpose	
Readers	
Organisation of text	Order of information:
Features	Language used for: 　　background facts 　　reporting what was said 　　speculating about the future

d In pairs, make a list of other types of important public appointments that women could hold. Are there positions in your country that a woman has never held?

e Now, using the analysis from c) as your plan, write your answer to the Portfolio task above. Use some of the examples that you thought of in d) as examples.

2 With a partner, plan how you would answer the example portfolio tasks below. Use the features of an article above to think about how you would answer the task.

1

'It is better to have brothers and sisters than to be an only child'. Write an article for a sociology magazine, explaining to what extent you agree or disagree with this statement. Support your point of view with relevant examples from your own childhood. (ISE II Portfolio Task 2010)

2

Write an article for a magazine called 'Star Sign' about a horoscope which came true for one of your friends. Say what was predicted and what actually happened. Conclude with your opinion on the reliability of this kind of prediction. (ISE II Portfolio Task 2010)

105

writing file

Creative and descriptive writing – story, diary, description
ISE II Controlled Written (approx. 250 words), Portfolio Section 3 (170-200 words)

Tasks in this section often involve both narrative, i.e. telling the story of what happened, and description, i.e. information and details about things, places and people in the story.

Purpose (examples)	• to narrate an experience (real or imaginary) • to describe a thing/place/person/event
Typical readers	• a friend or member of your family
Organisation of text	• flexible, for narrative stories events often appear in chronological order • diary entries often begin with *Dear Diary*, and end with a signature • descriptions of places could take the reader from one side to another or from front to back as if looking at a picture • descriptions of people could talk about how they look, features of their personality or how they speak and thinks they like to do • descriptions of events can be like stories
Features	• if describing events chronologically, sequencers are often used (*when*, *until*, *before*, etc.) • language will vary, according to experience being related, e.g. past tenses for a past experience, conditionals and modals to relate an 'ideal' or 'dream' experience

One type of task in this section could be to write a **diary entry**. This will include a story but looks a little like a letter at the beginning.

1a Put the paragraphs of the diary entry on page 107 in the right order to provide a version of the following task (the first paragraph has been done for you).

You have been working as a doctor in a busy hospital for one week. Write your diary at the end of your first week, describing the highlights and challenges of your new job and saying how you have been feeling.
(ISE II Portfolio task 2010)

Writing file

25th June 2010

Dear Diary,

[1] Well, it's the end of week one and I am exhausted! They said it was going to be hard but no one can prepare you for your first week.

[ ] At the end of the week, we had a meeting about our first impressions. Everyone was complaining about how tired they were. But we were all looking forward to our next week. It certainly makes such a change working as a 'real' doctor rather than a student.

[ ] After the first two days, they gave us more responsibility. I was in charge of six patients in the children's ward. It is sad and tiring at times. There is nothing worse than seeing a child crying and not being able to do much about it.

[ ] The week began slowly with an introduction to the staff and the ward. They are a great group of people. Helen, the head nurse, was very helpful and welcoming. The other first-year interns are great fun. Although there is a serious and efficient atmosphere, there is still time for chats and a joke now and again over lunch or a coffee.

[ ] For example, one boy came in with a broken arm. Although he wasn't in pain, he couldn't stop crying from the shock and there was nothing more that we could do for him after his arm was in the cast. He had to stay overnight and it was the first time he had been away from his parents so it was really hard for the lad.

Rajeev

b Read the text again and answer the following questions with a partner.

1 What challenges did Rajeev face?
2 What words in the text describe how Rajeev was feeling?
3 How is the text organised?
4 How many words can you find that refer to time and help order the story?
5 There is a mix of past and present tenses used in the text. What is the past tense mostly used for? What is the present tense used for?

Another type of writing task in this section is **a description**. It could be a description of anything, for example, a place, person or an event.

2a Read the answer to the portfolio task on page 108. Can you complete the gaps in the text (1-5) with the correct answer (A or B)?

1 A returned   B returning
2 A had   B have
3 A use to have   B used to have
4 A use to walk   B used to walk
5 A wasn't   B weren't

107

writing file

Imagine you had spent a day at school one hundred years ago. Write a description for the website www.schooldays.com describing your day. Say what people used to do at school and whether learning was easier or harder than it is today. (ISE II Portfolio task 2010)

SCHOOL A CENTURY AGO

I've just [1].................. from a day at school one hundred years ago. Kids [2].................. it so easy today compared to then.

The morning started early. Mum didn't [3].................. a car in those days so I had to walk to school over one mile away with my other forty classmates. There weren't as many schools then so children [4].................. long distances and fight for attention in much larger classes. Students of different ages were often mixed together as there [5].................. enough teachers.

The classroom was small and cold with wooden desks and chairs. There was a piano at the back of the class, which the teacher used to play and we'd sing. There was a platform at the front for the teacher to stand on and a huge blackboard with the alphabet written across the top. The room smelled of chalk and dust and was very noisy with the sound of shoes and bags on the hard wooden floor.

I was given my own small blackboard to practice my writing and maths and had to give it back at the end of the day. No pens or paper. They were too expensive. And no calculators or computers either. They hadn't been invented. This made things much harder as you couldn't look at what you had done in the last class to help you remember.

We are lucky that we don't study in the classrooms of one hundred years ago.

b Remember to answer the questions in the task. The task above asks the writer to say:
- what people used to do **and**
- whether learning was easier or harder.

Can you identify places in text that do the two things above?

c Descriptions can be made more interesting if they appeal to the readers' different senses. This helps to make the story come alive. In the description above what does the writer: see, feel, hear, smell?

3 In pairs, use the examples to plan one of the tasks below.

1

Imagine you have just appeared on a reality television show. Write your diary describing what happened and what the positive and negative aspects were. Say how your life would have been different if you had not appeared on the show. (ISE II Portfolio task 2009)

2

Write a short story for a writing competition about a young woman who did not use to believe in miracles until something incredible happened which changed her mind. (ISE II Portfolio task 2010)

3

Imagine you had a machine that could transport you through time and space. Write a description for a science-fiction magazine explaining where you would you go and what time you would you choose. Say what you could do there. (ISE II Portfolio task 2010)

Writing file

Skills for Reading into Writing – summarising
ISE II Controlled Written Section 1 – Reading into Writing (approx. 250 words)

> In the Controlled Written examination, the first task, Reading into Writing, will ask you to write an article or report based on information or ideas from a text.

1a Read this task and sample answer.

Read the text below and then, in your own words, write an article (approximately 250 words) for a social studies publication:

i) *summarising the reasons why the writer thinks that British people's values with regards to money have changed* **and**

ii) *expressing your own feelings about the importance of honesty in today's world.*

(ISE II Controlled Written Examination 2009)

> **How times have changed**
>
> Do you remember a time when a person who found a wallet full of cash in the street would do his best to find its owner and return it? In other words, do you remember a time when people were mostly honest?
>
> It was reported in a newspaper recently that people queued around the block at a cash machine when they heard that it was giving out as twice as much money as requested. But the papers did not suggest there was anything wrong in this mass bank robbery. On the contrary, they seemed to encourage the robbers' behaviour.
>
> Certainly [1] <u>a cash machine is an impersonal thing</u>. To steal money from it is not like stealing an old lady's handbag. But it is theft all the same.
>
> One onlooker, who didn't appear to be taking money out of the machine himself, nevertheless supported the robbers. 'It makes up for all the bank charges and I'm sure the greedy bank won't miss the money', he said.
>
> This suggested one of the reasons why those queuing up at the cash machine did not feel at all guilty about their crime. [2] <u>People don't trust banks</u> and [3] <u>they believe that banks overcharge them</u>.
>
> But there is more to it than that. There is a general feeling that [4] <u>money is now mainly obtained by luck rather than effort</u>. The fact that this may involve dishonesty is not a consideration, as long as there is little risk of being caught.

Part (i) asks you to **summarise the reasons for a change in values**. To write a summary, you need to capture the ideas you are asked for and write them in your own words.

b Match the reasons for a change in values (A–E) below with the reasons underlined in the text (1–4). There is one extra that you don't need.

A ☐ People rely on chance to make money rather than applying their skills.
B ☐ There is a lack of trust in banks.
C ☐ A cash machine isn't a person.
D ☐ People don't care about fellow citizens anymore.
E ☐ People feel that banks charge too much for their services.

c It is important that you use your own words, so use words with similar meanings. The reasons above (A–E) are similar to the text but use different words. Identify the different words used in each case.

For example, *In A the writer uses the words 'luck' while the statement uses 'chance'.*

d Now use the new words (A–E) and complete the sample task by i) summarising the text and ii) expressing your own feelings about honesty in today's world.

109

appendix 1 — Portfolio feedback form

Student portfolio feedback form

Candidate name: .... ISE 0 ☐ ISE I ☐ ISE II ☐ ISE III ☐ ISE IV ☐

Teacher name: .... Date: ....

Task section: .... Centre (name or number): ....

Teachers are strongly recommended to give candidates feedback in the preparation of their portfolios.

Teachers should complete just one copy of this sheet for each task presented by the candidate. It should be completed by ticking appropriate items in the right-hand column. This sheet must be the only form of feedback between teacher and candidate. When completed, this form should be handed to the candidate.

The candidate must ensure that it is attached to the final version and included in the portfolio.

Advice to the student	✓
Task fulfilment	
Parts of the task have not been completed — look at the instructions again	
The task does not meet the requirements set — look at the instructions again	
This work does not appear to be entirely your own — you must choose a different task	
Your work contains some irrelevant details and/or repetition	
You should add some more ideas	
You should give more description	
The format, style and/or register are not appropriate to the task	
The task is too long/short — check the word length range	
Organisation	
Your presentation and/or layout need to be improved	
You should check and improve paragraphing	
You need to add an introduction	
You need to add a conclusion	
You need to rewrite the task with more legible handwriting or word-process your work	
Grammar	
You need to check and improve the grammar of your work	
You should use a greater range of grammatical structures	
You need to check your word order	
Vocabulary	
You should use a greater range of vocabulary	
You need to check you are using the correct words	
Spelling/Punctuation	
You should check the spellings of words in your work	
You should check and improve the punctuation in your work	

Note: This form has been created as an example. See the Trinity College syllabus for the original form.

Grading & marks — appendix 2

1 How is my interview graded?

Pass grades: **A** – Distinction, **B** – Merit, **C** – Pass   Fail grade: **D**

2 How does the examiner assess my interview?

For **Grades 7** and **8** and **ISE II** you must fulfil the task in each phase of the interview – the Topic and discussion, Interactive task and Conversation. (See Trinity Syllabus for communicative skills, grammatical, lexical, and phonological items for each level.)

In addition she/he will look at fluency and promptness of response for the level.

3 How is my Portfolio and Controlled Written exam work in ISE II graded?

A – Excellent, **B** – Good, **C** – Satisfactory, **D** – Almost satisfactory, **E** – Not satisfactory

4 What is the examiner looking for in my Portfolio and Controlled Written exam tasks?

You must fulfil the tasks by using a range of appropriate vocabulary and grammar used accurately. Your writing must be organised coherently, with accurate spelling and punctuation.

5 How are my marks calculated?

The final marks are calculated and then confirmed in London, see below for weighting.

		Task within component	Component within the exam
ISE II Controlled Written exam	Task 1 Task 2	50% 50%	30%
ISE II Portfolio	Correspondence task Factual writing task Descriptive/creative writing	20% 40% 40%	20%
ISE II Interview	Topic Interactive task Discussion of Portfolio and conversation	33% 33% 33%	50%
Grades 7 and 8	Topic Interactive task Conversation	33% 33% 33%	100%

6 What percentage do I need to get in total to pass the exam? And what about passing with Merit or Distinction?

Pass – 65%   Merit – 75%   Distinction – 85%

7 What happens if I don't get a pass grade in one part of the exam?

In **Grades 7** and **8**, you will be able to use look-up tables to convert grades to Pass/Fail, there won't be any more numerical grades.

In **ISE II**, to get an overall pass grade, you must get a pass in both parts of the exam.

8 If I get a fail result, will the examiner tell me why?

Yes. The report indicates areas for improvement under these headings: communicative skills, grammar, lexis and phonology.

in compliance with the UNI EN ISO 9001:2008 standards for the activities of «Design and production of educational materials» (certificate no. 02.565)

Internet: www.blackcat-cideb.com
email: info@blackcat-cideb.com

Editors: Joanna Burgess, Maria Grazia Donati
Book and cover design: Maura Santini
Page layout: Veronica Paganin, Annalisa Possenti
Illustrations: Giovanni Da Re
Design coordinator: Simona Corniola
Picture research: Alice Graziotin

Art Director: Nadia Maestri

Picture Credits
t: top   c: centre   b: bottom   r: right   l: left
Cideb Archive; Brian Harkin/Getty Images News: 34tc; Matt Cardy/Getty Images News: 38l; Getty Images: 38r; George Stroud/Getty Images: 60tc; Jason Merritt/Getty Images:60cr; Jon Furniss/Getty Images: 63.

We would like to thank VSO for their kind permission to use material from their website in the article on page 58.

© 2011 Black Cat Publishing, Genoa, London

First edition: January 2011

Every effort has been made to trace the copyright holders and we apologise in advance for any unintentional omissions. We would be pleased to insert the appropriate acknowledgement in any subsequent edition of this publication.
All rights reserved. No part of this publication may be reproduced, stored in a retrieval system, or transmitted, in any form or by any means, electronic, mechanical, photocopying, recording or otherwise, without the previous written permission of the publisher.
The publisher reserves the right to concede authorisation for the reproduction of up to 15% of this publication upon payment of the established fee. All requests for such authorisation should be forwarded to AIDRO (Associazione Italiana per i Diritti di Riproduzione delle Opere dell'Ingegno), Corso di Porta Romana, 108 – 20122 Milano – email segreteria@aidro.org; www.aidro.org

In accordance with DL 74/92, the use of any commercial brand images and/or logos in this text is purely illustrative and should in no way be interpreted as endorsement on the part of Black Cat Publishing of such products and/or brands.

Printed in Italy by: Stamperia Artistica Nazionale, Trofarello, Turin

Reprint	II	III	IV	V	VI
Year	2012	2013	2014	2015	2016